The Book of the V2 2-6-2s

Includes the V4s

By Peter Coster
C.Eng, MICE, MCIT

Copyright IRWELL PRESS LIMITED
ISBN 10-1-903266-93-9
ISBN 13 978-1-903266-93-9

First published in the United Kingdom in 2008
by Irwell Press Limited, 59A, High Street, Clophill,
Bedfordshire MK45 4BE
Printed by Konway Press

CONTENTS

The rear end of COLDSTREAMER, I think more likely at Darlington than Doncaster, awaiting her tender after repair. The injector looks new, but the rear beam of the dragbox has already gained an encrustation of rust and scale by comparison with No.4801 on page 14. The bucket seats are not yet fixed, and the absence of AWS or its predecessor ATC suggests that the date is early in the 1950s. One of the two retaining chains can be seen, together with the opening to take the drawbar. The variety of brake and steam heating pipes, together with the drawbar and chains, were the reason why attaching and detaching the tender was not a five minute task! Note also the use of snap head rivets introduced by Edward Thompson: while these lacked the smooth finish of the countersunk rivets, they were slightly stronger and more economical to use.

PREAMBLE

In the years immediately after the 1939-45 war the Gresley era was symbolised daily not so much by the memory of his magnificent A3s and flying A4s, now enduring hard times, but by the numbers of unnamed, filthy black and inevitably anonymous large engines seen daily at work in their place on all manner of duties. The Pacifics, immediately after the 1939-45 war, were run down. Repairs had been carried out under the pressure of wartime using inferior materials, and the quality of fuel supplied had fallen, never to recover its pre-war level. New Pacifics began to appear, but the Gresley favourites looked shadows of their former selves. The anonymous and unnamed large engines looked very much like A3s, but there was a sense of youthful disappointment as they drew near, the quicker and often variable beat and the lack of a name confirming the worst.

Later, the advent of an ABC, purchased with hard-earned pocket money, revealed all. These were the V2s, widely referred to as the engines that won the war, at least on the LNER, the famous 'Green Arrows'. They were universally popular, smooth riding, economical, free steaming and with a rare turn of speed, and they were the LNER's all-purpose standby. I heard few drivers speak against them, although the introduction of self-cleaning screens certainly taxed vocabularies, and as a result there was the occasional rogue engine that defeated the crew for steam. The V2s were not always blessed with the finest of maintenance or fuel, and the sound of the exhaust, with the locomotive's 2:1 gear in far from pristine condition, became almost the signature tune for the old LNER. It is preserved forever on the superb recordings of night freight on the Waverley route by Peter Handford. It was regarded by engineers from the other Regions as certain proof of the unreliability of Gresley's conjugated gear.

The story of the V2s is comparatively short, but the engines themselves leave a rich store of memories with us. I have included some appendices illustrating the daily operation and showing the contribution from the V2s. This book is about the V2s, and illustrates many of the class at work and on shed. I have also included a short section on the V4, Gresley's last design, very much orphans in a Thompsonian storm.

So far, I have managed to illustrate each of the locomotives in the studies of the LNER Pacifics, most in their various forms over the years. I think that now, with 184 in the class, I must admit defeat. There are those locomotives that were always about and there are those like the elusive SPARROW HAWK which were camera shy. With nearly six V2s for each A4 the

York's first V2, No.4772, in the shed yard probably in 1936-37.

Nos.4782 and 4810 (60811, 60839) provide a stern test of the new down independent goods line bridge over the Yorkshire Ouse at Skelton in 1940-41. Notice that already the 'stepped' tenders have started to move around the class.

problem is of a different order. About one sixth of the class has escaped us, though no doubt they are out there somewhere.

I acknowledge the assistance that I have received from many good friends over the years, especially George W Carpenter, Peter Townend and Malcolm Crawley, and Dr. Geoffrey Hughes. My old friend of many years Canon Brian Bailey has made his collection of logs and photographs available to me as well, and I am particularly grateful to Chris Nettleton. The LNER archive, particularly that focussed on the V2s and V4s, has been freely consulted, principally the Part 6C of the LNER Locomotive Survey of the RCTS and W B Yeadon's Registers which by now have become the Old and New Testaments for most enthusiasts of an LNER persuasion. John Clay and Joseph Cliffe wrote a fine book on the LNER 2-8-2 and 2-6-2 classes many decades ago, and I would commend this strongly to anyone who can locate a copy nowadays.

This is the fourth detailed study of the large express steam locomotives of the LNER, setting out their history and work, discussing and commenting on their design, inevitably with a fair degree of hindsight and supported by the publisher's high standards of illustration and production. It will be the last in this form, simply because my experience and knowledge of other designs on the LNER and of the other 'three' is not of the same standard.

Lastly I would express my thanks to my wife, Su, for her help in supporting a husband who has written these curious books for curious people (in her eyes), about a time that is fast becoming ancient history!

Peter J Coster
Vice President, Gresley Society Trust,
Pendoggett Farm,
Bodmin,
Cornwall.

GREEN ARROW at Top Shed on May 8th 1954. Photograph M.N. Bland, www.transporttreasury.co.uk

A V2 footplate, specially prepared for the photographer. The sight of new or ex-works Type 3 D6900 and the front of another suggests to me that the date is late or even after the steam era, and the locomotive is the preserved one. A3 and A4 Pacifics were identical with the V2s. Strangely there is no AWS fitted, so the locomotive is only part restored for main line running.

CHAPTER ONE
DEVELOPMENT

The story of the design and construction of the V2 goes back to the end of Gresley's tenure of office with the Great Northern Railway. He had developed the Ivatt 0-6-0 into a splendid Class H3 2-6-0, and having perfected his conjugated valve gear in 1918 with his prototype three cylinder 2-8-0, went on in March 1920 to produce GNR No.1000, a powerful three cylinder 2-6-0, the first of GNR Class H4. Mixed traffic was not a motive power classification in those days and suitable designs were used on the various types of work. The H4 was the first GNR/ LNER mixed traffic locomotive.

Class H4 became the LNER Class K3, and eventually 193 locomotives were built to the K3 design. The K3 was noted principally for its huge 6ft diameter Diagram 96 boiler, which was the largest parallel boiler used on a conventional steam locomotive class on the LNER, possibly in the whole of the UK. Gresley's predecessor Henry Ivatt regarded the locomotive's capacity to boil water as paramount. Gresley was of the same mind; indeed in his K3 he upstaged Ivatt.

They were, more importantly, strong and free-steaming engines that took over the haulage of much of the LNER's faster freight and were also used on secondary passenger services. In 1921, the miners' strike caused the timetables to be changed so that fewer but heavier services remained. The K3s could time the 600 ton trains between London and Doncaster, and speeds up to 70-75mph were noted.

While the K3s were very capable locomotives, it had been clear from the outset that they could be wild-riding engines at speed. They were able to handle almost anything, and at low speeds their riding was steady enough, but as the speed rose – and the K3 had a fair turn of speed – the riding became distinctly lively. If there was significant wear in the axleboxes or horns, especially on the rear coupled axle, transferring the coal from tender to firehole door became something of a problem. Not for nothing did the crews call them 'Jazzers'. Gresley's three cylinder classes that lacked a rear carrying axle were powerful engines, and all were lively if not wild riders, and in an area congested with firebox, ashpan and dragbox it was next to impossible to provide any means of stabilising the rear end.

One of the longest diagrams in later years for an Immingham K3 2-6-0 was working the fast fish trains from New Clee to East Goods Yard at Finsbury Park, 156 miles, and for nearly 80 miles from Werrington Junction the K3 had to keep out of the way of the evening expresses. That stretch was worked by Boston men, and one felt for their comfort as they raced into London at 60-70mph with the unmistakeable heavy aroma of cod, haddock and herring, etc, following in the slipstream. One could never be sure about freight timings since they contained an element of randomness unknown in the passenger operations, but on at least one notable occasion soon after 21.00, the Immingham K3 came racing triumphantly into London ahead of the expresses, the heavy 17.15 from Leeds with its A4, and the Heart of Midlothian with its top link Grantham A1. The surprised crew were treated to a cheer from the lineside. The Top Shed lodging turn to Hull, worked by a B1, occasionally produced a Hull K3 which appeared to have no difficulty in running nearly 200 miles up to East Goods.

If it was not clear to Gresley that something better was required on the faster turns, then I am sure the Locomotive Running Engineers would have made the point discreetly. All of the evidence pointed to a locomotive

The official photograph of GREEN ARROW as she entered service, with a straight nameplate and LNER number 4771.

An official picture of GREEN ARROW, head-on. The Doncaster allocation painted on the buffer beam was something that became standard practice in 1938. It was incorrect in fact, since 4771/60800 was never a Doncaster engine. It is difficult to tell because of the blocking-out, but the V2 monobloc casting was not absolutely symmetrical because of the placing of the middle cylinder piston valve.

The first incarnation of GREEN ARROW as LNER No.637, with a curved nameplate.

with a rear carrying axle to constrain movement at the rear. As a traction unit the K3 was fine, but as a vehicle something more was needed. Gresley had toyed with the articulation of the tender to the locomotive as a means of restraining its riding, and outline plans for a 2-6-4-4 were prepared. Experienced depot staff knew that tightening the coupling to the tender drum-tight restrained the riding, as was done with Peppercorn's A1s decades later. The 2-6-4-4 proposal was abandoned, and in its place a large 2-6-2 was substituted.

At the time the LNER was suffering badly from the countrywide recession in which coal revenues fell sharply. The decision to accelerate expresses was put into action in 1932, and it seems that a similar decision to accelerate freight had been taken. Both were far sighted decisions that bear the marks of Wedgwood's leadership. Would that the LNER's policy had been followed when the railways had plenty of fast freight!

At this time, Gresley was occupied with the P2 Mikado design, and it is clear that while it was nearly finalised, the ancillary details were not. Then the possibility of a high speed service, similar to that of the Deutsches Reischbahn between Hamburg and Berlin, and the necessary traction for the task was beginning to assume greater importance. The continuing problems with the P2s coming on top of all of his responsibilities must have irritated him.

The 1930 Locomotive Building Programme included 14 K3s, later amended to 20, and while there was no programme for 1931, the 1932 programme included 3 more K3s. It also included two improved K3s 'to work fast goods and excursion trains in the Southern Area'. All five were cancelled in June 1932. There was no programme for 1933, but the 1934 programme eventually agreed contained only 10 K3s and no reference to 'improved K3s'.

After a meeting of the Area Mechanical Engineers on October 3rd 1934 at which the outline V2 proposal was accepted, the Locomotive & Traffic Committee met on November 29th 1934 to approve a provisional 1935 Locomotive Building Programme with 35 K3s and 14 V2s. This was changed on February 21st 1935 to 31 K3s and 5 V2s. The exact shape of the V2 was undecided, but the order for the 5 from the 1935 programme was placed at Doncaster in April 1935. The design first looked like a smaller Mikado, but it was revised, mercifully in some respects, dispensing with the poppet valves and ACFI feed water heater. Although the double Kylchap was not essential so long as the engines were well maintained, with the BR emphasis on the use of self-cleaning apparatus the susceptible draughting of the V2 was impaired, indeed at times 'destroyed' might be a more accurate description in some cases.

The revised design appeared in August 1935 with a streamlined wedge front as used on the first A4. Despite the suggestion from the wind tunnel tests that the A4 front was likely to be completely successful as a means of smoke deflection, its performance in service was still a few weeks away. One might conjecture as to why, but the final design had a conventional appearance instead, a fine handsome look fully in the Gresley tradition. The streamlined cab of the A4 was retained, and the main steam pipes left the smokebox low down, giving the locomotive a very handsome appearance.

The design eventually built was clearly related closely to the A3, A4 and P2. The compact three cylinder layout drove on to the middle coupled axle, with Bert Spencer's 1926 design operated by Walschaerts valve gear, conjugated to drive the middle valve with the famous 2:1 gear. The Diagram 109 boiler was 17ft long, with a wide 41.25sq ft grate area. The rear carrying axle was mounted in Cortazzi axleboxes, while the pony truck featured Gresley's swing link suspension. The exhaust design was a simple single blastpipe in the typical Doncaster style similar to the A3s. Somewhat unusually, a large locomotive was coupled to the group standard 4200 gallon tender, which restricted the V2's ability to make longer runs without refuelling. 'Group Standard' was something of a misnomer since during tests the capacity of the tender was measured and found to have been overstated by nearly 400 gallons

Most of the tenders were new, but a number were fitted to Nos.4804-4814 (60833-60043) cascaded from other types and displaced by tenders from withdrawn locomotives. The 4,200 gallon Group Standard tender had raised side or 'coping' plates above the water tank, intended to prevent coal spillage and increase capacity. The Darlington version of the tender had coping plates that were stepped out ornamentally; this looked fine coupled to the NER classes but with the more modern Gresley types they had a dated look.

At the end of the 1920s the country had endured great financial difficulties, few companies more so than the LNER, and among the economies at that time was a decision to couple smaller 3,500 gallon tenders to some of the big 0-6-0s of classes J38 and J39. Over the distances operated and at the speeds travelled these locomotives needed neither a great water capacity nor water pick-up gear, and the displaced tenders were coupled to engines of Class D49 for a few years before it was realised that they, too, had no need of pick-up gear either. The D49s got tenders of a similar size from withdrawn NER locomotives, releasing eleven tenders (built in the late 1920s for the 0-6-0s) for new V2s. Although the tenders remained with the original V2s for years, as time wore on they migrated around the class. When a locomotive entered the Works, it was swiftly dismembered and its components sent to the specialist departments such as the Boiler Shop, Brass Shop, Tender Shop and so on. If the tender was complete it would be coupled to the next completed locomotive of the appropriate class for painting, etc, and not necessarily to the one it had arrived with.

The LNER's system of locomotive numbering was originally sensible, but new construction resulted in blocks of numbers being thrust at random into the list making little or no sense. Originally it was intended to number the first one 637, but when the first five V2s emerged from Doncaster Works in the second half of 1936, they were numbered 4771-4775.

Despite the emergence of the V2s, the LNER continued to build K3s, and the provisional 1936 programme, agreed in February 1935, provided for another 21, plus 23 V2s. The successive building programmes were as follows:-

February 21st 1935, 1936 Programme, K3 - 21, V2 - 23.
January 9th 1936, 1936 Programme, K3 - 10 extra, V2 - 5 extra.
October 29th 1936, 1936 Programme, V2 - 11 extra.

Actually the total programme was further increased by another 28 V2s as part of the Government New Works

Programme. Thirty-three locomotives had been ordered before the first batch had been started at Doncaster, demonstrating the faith of the LNER management in their CME. In October and November 1936 it was increased further by no less than 39, making a total of 72 locomotives.

There was no 1937 or 1938 programme but in 1939 the agreed programme included 50 V2s, although only 46 were actually built before war broke out. The 1940 programme included 45 V2s. Under wartime conditions, authority for permitting locomotive construction was transferred to the Railway Executive Committee. The REC authorised material for the construction of another 25, although only 21 were built. The remaining four were taken by Edward Thompson, Sir Nigel Gresley's successor, to be built to a modified design eliminating the 2:1 conjugated gear. In September 1941 another 30 V2s were ordered, but a year later the order was cancelled. With Thompson committed to divided drive, it was hardly surprising. Summarising, the class of 184 locomotives comprised:

Programme	Quantity	Nos.	Builder
1935	5	4771-4775 (60800-4)	Doncaster
1936	23	4776-4798 (60805-28)	Darlington
1936 mod	5	4799-4803 (60829-32)	Darlington
1936 mod	11	4804-4814 (60833-43)	Darlington
1936 actual	28	4815-4842 (60844-71)	Darlington
1939	46	4843-4852 (60872-81)	Doncaster
		4853-4888 (60882-917)	Darlington
1940	45	4889-4899 (60918-27/38)	Darlington
		3641-3654 (60939-52)	Darlington
		3655-3664 (60928-37)	Doncaster
		3665-3674 (60953-62)	Darlington
1941	21	3675-3695 (60963-83)	Darlington

Construction of the 184 V2s followed at some distance in time behind the authorised programme, and building was not continuous as the manufacture of other designs and armaments took greater priority. One can see from the dates at which locomotives entered traffic that the number of gangs employed on construction varied as did the number of men in the gangs and on supporting production, when armament production took priority. A total of 118 had been put into traffic by the time of Gresley's death, and the remaining 66 were built under the stewardship of his successor, Edward Thompson. Although the latter opposed the use of the 2:1 gear which was a central feature of the V2, he had no alternative design to substitute until 1944. The last four V2s

were built to this alternative and emerged as A2/1s. The last V2, No.3695 (BR No.60983) did not leave Darlington Works until July 13th 1944.

The first V2 was named GREEN ARROW when it entered service. Originally numbered 637, it was fitted with curved nameplate when completed, but minds were changed, and when she emerged as No.4771, a straight nameplate was fixed to the smokebox. There was no naming policy for the new class, and the rapid increase in class size outstripped any possible supply of winning racehorses or fowls of the air, had it been considered. However, six of the class were selected for naming at random when newly built, oscillating between the Royal Scots of the LMSR and the Schools of the SR. Four were named after famous regiments or their nicknames and two after famous public schools. Another school declined the honour, and two decades later, a fifth regiment was added. The engines and the dates of their naming were (see table at bottom of page).

It was normal practice in mechanical engineering to attach a plate giving the details of the builder, type and date, whether it was a steam locomotive or a winch. In that way the relevant records, design and production drawings could be identified and referred to if necessary. One of the curiosities of the V2 class is that Darlington Works did not allocate works numbers to the engines on a consistent basis. 1,891 steam and 11 electric locomotives were built there until construction of the 1941 Building Programme started in 1942. Only the first 555 were given works numbering and from accounts of other classes built there, the use of works numbers ceased and presumably the running numbers were used instead. A large brass works plate was fitted, surprisingly given wartime metal priorities. Photographs of newly built Darlington V2s reveal a Doncaster type works plate, but close inspection shows that it bears only the running number and date in addition to the works name. The 1941 V2s and later construction of the A2/1s, B1s and A1s did have works numbers restarting at No.1903, so clearly there was a recording system in-house.

No.4780 (60809) THE SNAPPER (September 11th 1937)
No.4806 (60835) THE GREEN HOWARD (September 24th 1938)
No.4818 (60847) St. PETER'S SCHOOL, YORK AD 627 (April 3rd 1939)
No.4831 (60860) DURHAM SCHOOL (June 15th 1939)
No.4843 (60872) KINGS OWN YORKSHIRE LIGHT INFANTRY (May 20th, 1939)
No.4844 (60873) COLDSTREAMER (June 20th 1939)
No.60964 (3676) THE DURHAM LIGHT INFANTRY (April 29th 1958)

The selected V2 that remained unnamed was:-
No.4804 (60833) THE ROYAL GRAMMAR SCHOOL, NEWCASTLE UPON TYNE, AD 1545.

York's first V2, No.4772 in the shed yard at Grantham probably in 1936-7. Photograph (Revd A C Cawston Collection, Canon Brian Bailey).

Gateshead's No.884 is about to leave Grantham for the north in December 1946 soon after being fitted with a modified pony truck. (Revd A C Cawston Collection, Canon Brian Bailey)

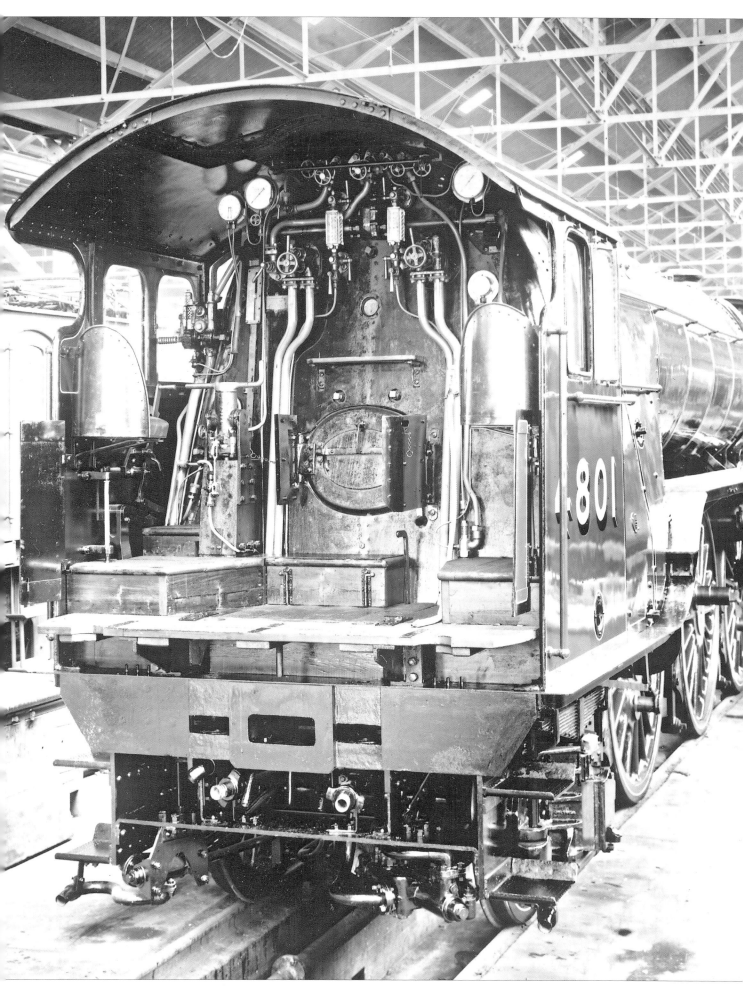

No.4801 (60830) nearing completion at Darlington Works in April 1938. I am unfamiliar with the layout of the works, and the absence of an overhead crane suggests that it is the Paint Shop. The locomotive would not have been painted until virtually complete and here only the motion needs to be erected and the valve gear set.

CHAPTER TWO
HINDSIGHT

The V2s, for the generation of railwaymen that had to serve during the 1939-45 war, acquired an enviable reputation as the locomotives that won the war. They were large, strong, economical and would keep going in the most desperately poor condition. Therefore, looking back at their introduction, any adverse conjecture about the V2s tends to sound blasphemous to the ears of many with LNER affections.

With the LNER's wish to replace life-expired locomotives with the new, large mixed traffic class, a relatively huge number had been ordered. I wish that I could believe that this was the act of a prudent Government anticipating hostilities, but it would be so far from the national character that I think that it had more to do with short-term political objectives! As it happened, when the building programmes came to fruition, the arrival of the new locomotives can scarcely have been more fortuitous, coming at a time when the balance of hostilities could have easily resulted in German replacing English in school curriculums. However, looking at the LNER in the mid-1930s, one can ponder the situation as it then was, and it is relevant to ask whether the V2 was quite what was needed.

When the LNER and LMSR are compared and contrasted, a fundamental difference emerges. Control of the Motive Power Department, as it later became, was the responsibility of the Chief Operating Officer in each case, although technical control remained with the CME. In the case of the LMSR the Chief Operating Officer exercised final authority over the Building Programme, whereas on the LNER it remained with the CME. With many pre-Grouping designs in their last years, a design with a wider route availability than RA9 was required, and with fewer complications, bearing in mind the lower standard of maintenance prevailing at lesser depots. William Stanier's Black Five 4-6-0 was smaller and less powerful, but a better answer operationally. Edward Thompson's two cylinder, smaller wheeled 'Sandringham', the B1 4-6-0, was the excellent answer to many of the LNER's problems, belatedly.

Locomotives with no rear carrying axle tended to wear more heavily at the rear, due to the lateral forces induced by the cyclic piston thrusts at the front and the lack of lateral cushioning at the rear. Three cylinder locomotives were better in that respect. It was next to impossible to include some design feature exerting horizontal control at the rear due to the presence of the grate and ashpan, together with the strengthening of the frames around the drawbar. This was why the Cortazzi design appealed as a neat and effective answer to the need for control at the rear. As a result, most 4-6-0s, and probably 4-4-0s as well, could impart a vigorous, if not downright rough, ride when worn. The B1 was an excellent locomotive but, as speed rose, the riding grew rougher as with all steam engines and above 65-70 mph (I was told) the vibration and rough riding even with a modest mileage, could be hard on the crew. Cut-offs shorter than 20% would

No.3645 at Darlington, probably in 1942. Her derailment at Hatfield precipitated the modification of the V2 pony truck design. No.60943, as she became, was a GN engine. Although there is no trace of works numbers for any but the last twenty V2s built at Darlington, as mentioned in the text, No.3645 has a Doncaster style works plate on the smokebox. It confirms that works numbers were not used; although Doncaster-type works plates were fitted, they carried the running number.

result in a distinctly rough and noisy ride. The late Bill Harvey at Norwich recognised this fact. When a B1 had over 50,000 miles to her credit, it became progressively more difficult to get drivers to take her. So he invested precious artisan time in taking the rear down and renewing the trailing coupled axleboxes: as a result the engine could run over 100,000 miles with relatively tolerable riding. Even the Black Five, an excellent locomotive regarded by those of a maroon affection as the panacea, could often give an abominable ride when badly run down. However, one of the most famous classes for lively riding was the Ivatt Large Atlantic; these *did* have a carrying rear axle, which shows the perils of generalising!

Knowing all this, one could appreciate Gresley's reluctance to dispense with the rear carrying axle that had performed well on the A1 and A3 Pacifics, especially since his own designs without a rear axle (as already mentioned) were vigorous riders if not worse when worn – the K2s, K3s and B17s. Three cylinders and conjugated valve gear were almost a standard feature on Gresley's designs. It was considered unnecessary to use a bogie since the pony truck appeared to have served well on the K3s, P1s and P2s, and length was a consideration. A 2-6-2 wheel arrangement thus emerged from the deliberations at Doncaster. Use of 5ft

8in coupled wheels in a smaller design would have required either the Diagram 100 parallel B17 boiler, or a new design of tapered boiler. Interesting, but Gresley evidently preferred a slightly larger machine. Using 6ft 2in wheels would allow a shortened version of Doncaster's excellent standard Pacific boiler working at 220 psi. The disadvantages were that the V2 was too big and therefore too costly, but big was not a criticism as far as Gresley was concerned. However, its weight and size limited it to the route availability of the Pacifics, RA9, although they worked occasionally to Hull and Scarborough, and regularly over the Joint line from March to Doncaster via Lincoln. It was a great pity that they could not work over the GE main lines, since they would have transformed the service. It is a pity that the engineering departments could not cooperate to deal with the restrictions there.

It was a great pity that the smaller V4 2-6-2 which emerged five years later, a few months before the death of her designer, was unable to establish itself in the LNER's locomotive fleet. It was planned to order another 10 after the first two were built, but an unsympathetic successor and wartime priorities prevented the proposal from reaching the building programme. It was almost certainly a machine that was rather too intricate for the rough and tumble of the

mixed traffic world, but what little experience of the two small Prairies was gained showed that they were remarkable machines, capable and economical. A pity, for one could imagine them running the New Clee and Hull fast fish services effectively. One is forced to the conclusion that the LNER really needed a locomotive that was smaller than the V2 and larger than the V4, and less complicated than either. Within a few years the LNER had the design that was really needed, the B1, but in a rapidly changing world it had every reason to bless Gresley's memory.

Scotland's first V2, No.4775 (60804) of Tay Bridge shed, now fitted with a single line tablet changer. I think it is at Dundee. Photograph W. Hermiston, www.transporttreasury.co.uk

LNER 4795 was Top Shed's second V2 (60814) and is seen here by the Cenotaph (coaling plant) with her proud driver.

No.60834, always a Scottish engine, fresh from overhaul at Darlington. The absence of a shedplate and standard of finish suggests to me that the period is May 1948 when she was selected for repainting to demonstrate the new BR black livery.

CHAPTER THREE
ENGINEERING HISTORY

The works at Darlington and Doncaster, faced with the huge order for what was a large locomotive, turned the V2s out steadily. They had other orders to build, and there was a constant stream of worn locomotives that had been proposed and accepted for general overhaul. With the declaration of war, the railway companies' workshops were a vital source of engineering excellence for the manufacture of armaments, which took priority over all else. Nevertheless the railways had to continue running with a workforce depleted in numbers and skills, and almost certainly the quality of the repairs suffered from inferior material and attention. So it was not until 1944 that the last V2s were built, by which time the new CME had other ideas.

The Superheater Co. had a fairly close relationship with the LNER, and five V2s built in 1938, Nos.4804-4808, were fitted with that firm's Melesco multiple valve regulator. Little experience of the performance of this regulator was obtained since the five examples were removed during the war. This was probably due to lack of spares and a need to avoid detaining locomotives overlong

in the works waiting for replacement parts. The regulator was used by the BR central design team, and was fitted experimentally to 5 Peppercorn A2s successfully.

Edward Thompson's rebuilt Mikados and the last four improved V2s (Nos.3696-3699) established a common theme which was developed into his new Pacific, the A2/3. With the cessation of the war and the construction of A2/3s, it was decided by his successor, Arthur Peppercorn, to evaluate the new Pacific in comparison with the V2 of Sir Nigel Gresley. The Pacific was a significantly more powerful locomotive, and the tests are discussed in *The Book of the A1 and A2 Pacifics* in more detail, but frankly there was little about them which could not have been foretold by a discerning locomotive engineer. The tests took place in 1946 between Leeds and Newcastle with loads of roughly 350 and 450 tons, and Newcastle and Edinburgh with 435 tons.

The tests were carried out using the first A2/3, No.500 EDWARD THOMPSON and Gateshead V2 No.959. The programme was not very long, running the risk of gathering insufficient

reliable information to inform conclusions, but also the fuel used was very variable, nearly causing V2 No.959 to stop SOS (short of steam) on one occasion. The conclusion was that the Pacific was a much more powerful and free steaming engine, but on lighter loads the V2 was the more economical of the two. The report contained the useful advice that the Pacific should be kept to the heavier tasks where its large grate and greater strength could be used to advantage. For much of the time after 1951, motive power policy in the south was precisely the reverse, the A2/3s being used on short all stations services for much of their time, a duty well within the capacity of a B1 4-6-0 or even a 4MT 2-6-0.

In December 1946 Kings Cross V2 No.813 was the subject of an odd experiment in smoke deflection. Not that it had been a problem with the V2 class, since there was no suggestion that the V2 crews were ever troubled by ineffective smoke deflection. If anything, it was the A2/3 that presented deflection problems. Quite who ordered this experiment is not known. It followed a month after the comparative trials with

813, in a truly appalling state, externally at least, during 1948 before BR renumbering.

Above and left. **No.60813, at Kings Cross two months after modification with an unique smoke deflector.**

the A2/3, which suggests that the proposal was made by someone in authority, possibly outside the department. The chimney had the rim turned down to give it a plain shape, and a deflector fitted behind the chimney. The deflector strongly resembled the upturned rim of a firing shovel. I am unaware of any tests or reports with this engine, but it kept this odd arrangement for almost 20 years, even after being sent from one Region to another, Kings Cross to St.Margarets, along with 5 other V2s in 1951, undergoing eight changes of boiler during that period. There seemed to be no clear policy in this respect, for such odd modifications either survived as in this case, or were summarily removed at the first opportunity. I suppose a Works manager might have argued that nobody subsequently authorised its removal, so there it stayed.

During those dark wartime years, a problem arose with the V2s, hitherto a problem-free design. During the war, in 1944 a derailment occurred at Newark with a V2 on an up express. There was a blanket PSR (Permanent Speed Restriction) of 60mph in force, but the condition of the permanent way generally had degenerated and there were many poor patches. This was thought to be the cause. A number of accidents occurred involving V2s, none of which were attributed to bad riding, but in February 1946 No.4878 (60907) derailed at Thirsk, allegedly due to excessive speed. The up main at Thirsk is straight, not curved, but it did have a S&C (switches & crossings) layout which usually rode poorly, sometimes worse. Then, on July 15th 1946, No.3645 (60943) derailed near Hatfield at 60mph with the down Aberdonian and on November 10th, No.905 (old 4876) was derailed at Marshmoor with the evening Newcastle-Kings Cross express.

In each case the track was thought to be the principal cause of derailment. Such matters were investigated by a Joint Enquiry, chaired by a District or Divisional officer, where a full and frank exchange of views could be relied on as each engineer and operator defended his corner. It was great fun if one was 'in the clear' as it were, to sit back and watch others slug it out. Incidentally, no Joint Enquiry that I attended was completed without the assembled company uncovering some illicit practice introduced by the staff to simplify their day. For example on the SR it was commonplace for drivers to be relieved at Fratton rather than Portsmouth, so that on one occasion the miscreant who started away against the platform starter's danger aspect was not the nominated driver, who by that time was merrily speeding home to the arms of his – or someone else's – loved one!

The track was surveyed in close detail after an accident, and it was very rare to find it the acme of perfection at the point of derailment in such cases. As a civil engineer, I remember – vividly – having one's track survey there for the world to judge, and judgment was easy. Derailments usually happen when a susceptible wheelset encounters substandard track as at a railjoint or over a wet patch. The vital consideration was whether the track was just poor, or poor enough to cause a derailment. The vehicle's compliance with the mechanical engineer's design was measured (statically) but the dynamic performance of the vehicle and wheelset remained largely unknown since in pre-electronic days there was no reliable means of checking. I recall a derailment of a train of (fortunately) empty bogie oil tanks on a length of track which was poor, but the bogie design was incapable of coping sufficiently quickly with changing track cross-levels that were undesirable, though within tolerance. If vehicles derailed on every track imperfection it would be impossible to run the railway. At the Joint Enquiries of 1946, I would imagine that the CCE tired of being blamed for all derailments, and the upshot was that the CME, faced with the mounting evidence that his locomotives were liable to fall off the track too easily at every imperfection, conceded that the riding of the V2 pony truck was not all that it should have been.

The swing link design was self-centring, partly inherently, and partly because the swing of the links tended to lift the front of the locomotive. The self-centring action was intended to steer the locomotive into and out of a curve. As the imposed weight on the pony truck could rise to 12 tons, the swing links and pins wore rapidly, a problem worsened by poor lubrication, so that any self-centring action soon diminished, leaving the truck to hunt and the main coupled wheelbase to hit curves without adequate steering from the pony truck. As all of the derailed V2s were built in wartime conditions it might have been worth checking on the quality of the material used. Edward Thompson had encountered the same problem with the Mikados, and had replaced the pony truck with a bogie. Where he had used a pony truck on his L1 and K1, it was with horizontal spring control.

The CME, Arthur Peppercorn, and his staff seem to have been harbouring doubts about the V2 pony truck, and in no more than four weeks, No.884 had a new truck of the type used by Edward Thompson. It owed much to the design used on the Stanier 8F, of which Doncaster built 50 and Darlington 53. The design was successful and the class was converted. The one feature that required amendment was the vertical springing, which was originally laminated. This proved unsatisfactory in service, since although the springing coped with imposed loads, where the track dropped momentarily under load as it would for example at a low railjoint, they were unloaded. The answer was the use of helical springing, in which the initial compression made them better able to respond to variations in track cross-level. Eventually all pony trucks were fitted with helical springs.

The quality of locomotive coal had fallen badly, producing more ash and char. Emptying the smokebox was important to prevent equipment malfunctioning and if the char continued to burn, the smokebox vacuum and hence the steaming would have been affected. It was a filthy and dangerous job with few handholds, and the char tended to get into the wrong places. An arrangement was devised whereby the particles in the exhausting gas were deflected around the smokebox by screens of heavy wire mesh until they were broken down sufficiently to be exhausted, or dropped to the bottom of the smokebox. It was called self-cleaning, but that was only partly true. The LNER fitted some V2s with the arrangement, and after some adjustment to the blastpipe diameter, it appeared to work adequately. The initial optimism was misplaced, and conversion was halted pending further action, as the steaming had been adversely affected.

With the new BR administration, the use of self-cleaning apparatus was encouraged. As a result, burnt smokeboxes seemed to become the norm since presumably they were not being emptied. A total of 24 V2s were fitted with a variety of screens and modified blastpipes. The ex-GWR engineer who became the Eastern Region's new M&EE, Kenneth J. Cook, decided to try Swindon exhaust proportions on four V2s involving a slightly enlarged chimney. No.60854 was fitted with a copper capped chimney in the process, but Cook was ordered to remove it promptly. Complaints about accessibility were soon received, and it was clear that the steaming had been adversely affected.

In May 1952, as a result of similar troubles with fitting the apparatus in three cylinder locomotives, it had been decided to send a V2 to Swindon for steaming tests. The engine selected was New England's No.60845, having run 8,000 miles since overhaul. This engine was regarded by many in the south as the black sheep of New England's considerable V2 fleet, and the view of some of the Eastern Region motive power engineers at the time was that Swindon will have done well if they could sort her out. This was the only occasion on which a large Gresley locomotive was indicated.

There didn't seem to be much that was right with No.60845. Early testing was held up by the V2 running hot, injectors failing and the brakes not acting promptly. The engine broke loose on the Test Plant and required repair. Once its faults had been corrected and the V2 was running, it was clear that the steaming of the engine was abysmal. What caused even greater concern were the indicator cards taken from the cylinders, which could hardly be believed. The disparity between the forward and return strokes of the cylinders was considerable, and indeed in the same cylinder the difference was astonishing. In some cases much less work was being done on the return stroke. O.S. Nock, a senior engineer with Westinghouse and a well-connected and experienced railway commentator, asked how on earth such an engine could actually run at all.

There is another view of all this. It must have been clear – or at least I hope so – to the engineer in charge of testing that No.60845 was seriously out of adjustment at least so far as valve setting was concerned. The tests should have been stopped then and there, and the V2 returned to Doncaster with some pungent comments. One might ask what point was there in testing a locomotive in such a defective condition, and what useful knowledge might have been gained? Also, as the V2 had been given a general overhaul a few months earlier at Doncaster Works, some particularly searching questions should have been asked there. An engine would not have been allowed back into traffic with the valves out of adjustment, and in any case she would have been returned from Carr Loco for adjustment had a mistake occurred. Coincidentally, among the photographs selected for this book is one taken on April 23rd 1952, two weeks after re-entering traffic from that particular general overhaul, showing No.60845 bringing a fast freight into Peterborough from the south. I would imagine the V2

The unique V2 60813 at Cambridge on May 1st 1950 when allocated to Kings Cross. Photograph M.N. Bland, www.transporttreasury.co.uk

was in good condition then, to have been rostered for such a duty, and yet within two weeks it was in a seriously defective condition. How, one might speculate, but the indicator diagrams suggest to me that by the time she had reached Swindon for testing the valve setting for the middle cylinder was badly out of adjustment. That is very strange considering the depth of experience with conjugated gear available at New England and the very good name Doncaster Works had for the quality of its valve setting. The valves on V2s can be set accurately to give an even beat, as witness GREEN ARROW when originally restored by Bill Harvey.

There seems to have been an extraordinary degree of partisanship at the time for some at a senior level and a readiness to re-fight old battles when the concern should have been to achieve the best for the future. No.60854's copper capped chimney may have been an expensive joke, but it betrayed something of the passions that still ruled in the mechanical engineering world. No doubt some enjoyed hugely the results of the Gresley conjugated gear being tested for the first time, showing it to be the unreliable and unsatisfactory arrangement that they believed that it was. The ghosts of the past were dead but wouldn't lay down.

The Swindon testing team at the time had the reputation of sharpening the exhaust in order to accelerate the exhaust jet and hence increase the draught on the firebed, but also increasing the back pressure in the cylinders, forcing the driver to use longer cut-offs and burn more coal. However, the evaporation rate was successfully raised from 14000lbs to 30000lbs/hr by altering the blastpipe proportions, a dramatic increase, and without increasing coal consumption significantly. The Swindon team were able to claim justifiably that they had indeed 'sorted No.60845 out'. No.60845 had been worked on a test train between Stoke Gifford (now Bristol Parkway) and Reading West with varying loads up to 762 tons and her performance, despite the wide variations in individual cylinder performance, was quite good. The V2, despite its size and rated tractive effort, was economical rather than powerful, and a peak IHP of 1870 was recorded in these tests.

The experiments with self-cleaning apparatus stopped in the mid-1950s. Any economy had to be set against the increased attention needed to examine and correct the equipment. As mentioned previously the V2s in many cases were running on poorer fuel and the amount of char produced must have been greater. The equipment was a major obstacle to boiler and superheater inspection and repair, and it was hardly a surprise that fitters 'forgot' to replace it after repairs. There were tales of

Doncaster or Darlington receiving a V2 for overhaul with the self-cleaning equipment missing, but the practice must have been fairly widespread since V2s were returned, overhauled, without the screens replaced. Some years later similar equipment was fitted as a spark arrestor only to find that steaming was adversely affected once more. One might wonder did they ever learn? One of the basic problems was the existence of 'Berlin Walls' within the BR organisation which deterred the Plant & Machinery Dept. from assisting their Motive Power brethren by mechanising the process of smokebox cleaning. One is forced to the conclusion that the result of a lot of time and money spent was the impairing of the steaming of a perfectly good locomotive.

The design of the single blast arrangements in the V2 seemed to continue the somewhat susceptible design of the Gresley A1 and A3 Pacifics. Steaming appeared to be strong and reliable before the 1939-45 war, but not after. The quality of the coal was said to be lower, and strong young men were reluctant to labour for a poor reward when better opportunities existed outside the railway industry. The steaming of all single blast Pacifics and V2s was no longer as sure and certain as it was, and guards were booking lost time against the locomotives far more often than would have been the case before the war.

Without doubt the 300 existing single blast locomotives should have been fitted with double Kylchaps there and then.

The V2 had a single monobloc casting that included the three cylinders and smokebox saddle together with all internal steam passages, which, after modification to overcome some weaknesses in the design, was very successful. It effected a saving in weight and avoided a number of steamtight joints, but the one casting was expensive. When it needed replacing because one worn or faulty cylinder could no longer be repaired, it was expensive. At a suggestion from Darlington, the casting was redesigned, split into three, so that only the middle cylinder (usually) needed replacing. While the change was sensible, saved money and worked perfectly well, one cannot help regretting the detraction from the fine racy lines of the original design. The new design brought the outside cylinder steam pipes outside the saddle, rather like the A3s, giving the engines a front-heavy look. 71 of the 184 V2s were converted in this way until in 1962, BR decided that the V2s could be condemned and their place taken by the newer Class 9F 2-10-0s pending full dieselisation.

The overhaul and repair of the V2s was shared between Doncaster (ER engines) and Darlington (NE and Scottish engines) until January 1957 when the volume of Pacific work at Doncaster led to the V2 class being dealt with at Darlington. One of the first Kings Cross V2s to return complete with separate cylinders was one of their best, No.60862, and a number of complaints followed, that she would not run as fast and freely as she had before. Other overhauled V2s drew similar complaints. No.60862 had her valves reset, and it was found that Darlington had set the valves cold, with no expansion allowance. In fact it was the general practice there, and had been for a long time, including the construction of the 23 A1s and four A2/1s there. Subsequently an allowance was introduced.

With the success of the conversion of the A4s and then the A3s to double Kylchap exhaust, even at this late stage in the steam era, conversion of the V2s seemed a sensible and logical step. Despite the fact that both conversions had been properly authorised and financed, those at the Centre were critical of the Regions in enacting a design alteration, and they took the proposal over. Two V2s were converted in early 1960, Nos.60817 and 60963. Prejudice was still alive and well at the Centre, and despite the success with the Gresley Pacifics, the conversions were not with double Kylchap but cheaper Royal Scot double blastpipes. Reports on both locomotives might have been described as underwhelming, the steaming not having been significantly altered. Since the orificial area of the twin 4in diameter blastpipes was much the same as the largest single blastpipe of the V2, it was hardly surprising. With the greater circumference of the double blast, the entrainment of smokebox gas may have been improved, but the loss of diameter due to charring from carbonised lubricating oil would have been greater.

Later in 1960, one V2, No.60881 was fitted with a double Kylchap and, as most engineers east of Marylebone expected, the transformation was remarkable. On a trial run down Stoke Bank the driver was instructed to ease the regulator to prevent the speed rising over 100 mph. The top speed has been quoted as 101.5mph, although doubts about this have been expressed, since sister V2 No.60880 has been associated with a similarly fast run down Stoke. In both cases no reliable evidence has emerged to support a claim of a three figure maximum. Maybe it was a speedometer reading, which was usually a little high. No three figure maximum properly supported by passing times and speeds recorded with a V2 has emerged over the years. As a result of the successful conversion, five further V2s were modified, Nos.60858, 60862, 60880, 60902 and 60903. Of the eight V2s fitted with double chimneys, only Nos.60862 and 60881 had separate cylinder castings. The two less successful conversions, Nos.60817 and 60963 retained the plain double blastpipes until withdrawal.

The justification for the last-minute conversions was the provision of

GREEN ARROW in BR black livery climbs toward Potters Bar with a down express in the late 1940s.

adequate piloting at Peterborough. The turntable would not accommodate a Pacific and good V2s were essential as the principal services were turning over to diesel power which was unreliable at that particular period. Famously, at a trade union meeting, Peter Townend was told that New England wanted more Kylchap V2s and not more diesels.

The Kylchap V2s were regarded as the equal of a Pacific, and they were highly regarded at a time when locomotive replacement was common-place. In the late 1950s Kings Cross 1A link, which worked the fast freights from and to London, took over 714down, the 16.15 Kings Cross York Dringhouses, returning from York the following day on 273up, the 00.30 from Inverkeithing.

Freight timekeeping was much less punctual than passenger, and the timekeeping of 714 was not good. It had to wait for the Tees-Tyne Pullman before entering the two track section at Digswell, and it was well north of Hitchin on two track sections before the evening expresses caught it. It either delayed the expresses, or was recessed and ran late as a result. Likewise 273up tended to get under everyone's feet including the Elizabethan in summer. It was a constant problem. Kylchap V2s not required for standing pilot were drafted on to it, and the problem disappeared overnight.

On one occasion a Deltic diesel had to be replaced on the down 'Bradford Flyer' – which by then had become the 'West Riding'. Now there was a time when a

V2 pilot was not always greeted with unalloyed enthusiasm, especially if the accrued mileage was high and the fire low, and even more especially if the diesel driver had surrendered his overalls for a new 'diesel' uniform. This time it was different, and the Kylchap V2 rose to the occasion magnificently. The pumping capacity of the much stronger exhaust made it possible to bring to the fire to white heat quickly, a characteristic of the double Kylchap, and the V2 made a magnificent climb to Stoke, passing the summit at 68mph with her 400 ton load. This must have entailed the V2 developing over 1800 IHP for most of the climb beyond Tallington, and 2100 IHP for the last three miles to the summit. Redraughting had increased the

maximum potential power by some 400 IHP.

The V2 as built was not quite such a powerful locomotive as one might think. It had the A4 'engine' with the same valves and cylinders, the same valve settings, much the same boiler but with a lower working pressure, the same grate and a similar single exhaust. The rated tractive effort reflected the lower working pressure. Yet while the maximum power output from a single chimney A4 was around 2,600 IHP, the only recorded maximum V2 IHP was the 1,870 IHP achieved by No.60845 on test at Swindon. There is no doubt that they could develop much the same power output as a single blast A3 but I think it is true to say that however fast they could

run, no sustained power output of any significance is on record with a V2. It would be nice to be proved wrong.

The lesson, as Swindon found some 80 years ago, is that tractive effort is only relevant in comparing haulage capacity at low speeds. It is difficult to overstate the importance of correct draughting, and the capacity of the front end layout to cope with very high steam flows is critical in developing high power. In my view both A3 and V2 designs suffered from the handicap of a poor exhaust design for coping with post-war fuel. However, the V2 was an oversized locomotive for its intended range of work, and the designers judged economy to be more important than power output. The East Coast main line

is fairly flat by comparison with others in the UK, and a powerhouse V2 was unnecessary. They performed their work with economy and comfort, and in creating his V2, Gresley showed the railway industry how useful a large mixed traffic locomotive might be. Bulleid on the Southern built his Pacifics, light and heavy, fondly known on the Southern as the 'Flannel Jackets, Water Closets and Beer Bottles'. BR followed his example with the Britannias which were effective and set new standards on the GE for performance and reliability.

Ferryhill's long-term resident, E819, at Haymarket in 1948. Photograph www.transporttreasury.co.uk

The official 1948 photograph of 60847 St. PETER'S SCHOOL, YORK at Darlington.

CHAPTER FOUR
OPERATION OVER THREE DECADES

PRE-WAR

The V2 incorporated the internal streamlining also used on the A4 Pacific introduced a year before. The advantages were of greater tractive power, economy, and a surprising turn of speed. But then, all of Gresley's locomotives, size for size, could go like the wind when required. In 1936, the first five were sent to Kings Cross, New England, York (2) and Dundee Tay Bridge. The two Southern Area V2s were soon appearing on summer extras, and their turn of speed impressed greatly. The prototype was named GREEN ARROW, after a premium fast freight service initiated by the LNER, and she became the regular engine for No.562 down, the No.1 speed fast freight for Leith Walk and Glasgow which departed at various times between 15.00 and 16.00. Post-war this was the famous No.266 down, the Scots Goods, and many thousands of tons were hauled northwards over the years by GREEN ARROW and her sisters before the Pacifics took over in September 1956.

The operating authorities needed no urging to capitalise on the versatility of the V2s and they were used on reliefs, excursions, parcels and of course fast freight. The V2s were a new concept in railway operating, the heavy mixed traffic locomotive. Only the GWR 4700 2-8-0s could be said to belong to that power classification at the time. Good as the 47XXs were, one would not put them on a principal service other than in an emergency. The V2s were allocated to depots with involvement in fast freight work in the main, but their allocation took them farther afield than their Pacific cousins. The full list of their depots over three decades is as below.

Ex-GNR
Kings Cross, New England, Grantham, Doncaster, Mexborough, Ardsley, Copley Hill, March, Wakefield (LMR).

Ex-GCR
Neasden, Woodford Halse, Leicester, Sheffield (Darnall), Gorton.

Ex-NER
York, Darlington, Thornaby, West Hartlepool, Gateshead, Heaton, Tweedmouth

Ex-Scottish Area
St.Margarets, Haymarket, Eastfield, Dundee Tay Bridge, Aberdeen Ferryhill, Perth and St.Rollox (LMS).

Curiously, neither Neville Hill nor Carlisle Canal had V2s for any length of time. No.4853 (60882) went to the latter shed when new for a month or so before moving to Edinburgh. One might have thought that the slightly higher tractive effort, smaller coupled wheels and better laid out front end would have suited the work there, but locomotive men could be conservative, and the Canal men liked their A3s. With large V2 fleets to plunder at nearby York and St.Margarets, presumably there was no need.

York and later St.Margarets, together with New England and Doncaster, had particularly large fleets. While indeed their weight hampered their wider use, there was very little a V2 could not manage. Their economy and comfort made them popular with crews who previously had to suffer the shortcomings of the 2-6-0s' riding and the pre-Grouping designs. They were particularly well received in Scotland, taking curvature, gradient and poor track smoothly and easily. While the same design of pony truck was used on the P2s and V2s, the shorter fixed wheelbase of the V2 made the riding easier. The greater tractive effort of the P2 was

Ouch! The mortal remains of 936, recovered from the wreckage caused by the collision outside Doncaster on August 9th 1947. The V2 was the train engine of the 13.25 Kings Cross-Leeds which ran into the rear of the 13.10 Leeds, with disastrous results. One would have thought that it would be quicker and cheaper to build a new engine as was done with GRAND PARADE in 1938: perhaps it was in all but name – or number.

New England's 60912 with an up Newcastle area express on the up main at Doncaster on June 27th 1956. Meanwhile on the up platform road, A1 KESTREL sets back on to the up Yorkshire Pullman.

valuable, but the V2 was strong at low speeds, and of course, critically, the fireman had a much smaller grate to deal with.

York's No.4782 (60811) was pressed into action twice in early 1938 replacing a failed A4 on the down Coronation, and in July the same shed's No.4773 (60802) relieved SEA EAGLE at Newark on the up train. Apart from a signal check at Stilton Fen, it kept time to Kings Cross. When SILVER FOX was failed at the last minute, the two-months old No.4789 took the down West Riding Limited on January 14th 1938. From the available information, the V2 must have reached Leeds having lost only four minutes on the hard schedule, averaging 66.7mph net, start to stop. The V2s appeared to be quite capable of maintaining the streamlined schedules when pressed hard. Doncaster used their V2s frequently on the Yorkshire Pullman in place of a Pacific, a prestigious service if not such a tightly timed one. The up service was allowed 155 minutes for 155.95 miles, and the V2s more than held their own with loads of 380-420 tons, including some flying descents of Stoke Bank. The Doncaster men were not averse to showing their southern colleagues a clean pair of heels.

WARTIME
By the time the 75th V2 had entered traffic in July 1939, the 1939-45 war was about to break out. The normal service was replaced with an emergency timetable in which passenger trains were drastically curtailed, in order to provide capacity for essential freight and troop movements. Some 60-70 years ago our armed services were many times greater in numbers and most movements were by rail. As a result, the remaining services increased to almost double length, and loads of over 20 coaches were commonplace. By Easter 1940, some trains had reached 25 and 26 coaches, making station handling very difficult. That seems to have been the absolute limit of the terminus at Kings Cross in train length for, down-country, stops were nearly always through stations where very large trains could be drawn up. Because of wartime restrictions on information gathering and publication much of the wartime operating remains unknown, but it is probable that the heaviest passenger train to be hauled in this country was hauled at this time by a V2. The event is well known. As the morning Newcastle express travelled south, it acquired additional coaches, until GLADIATEUR arrived at Peterborough with 26 coaches, 764 tons tare. The gross weight remains

unknown, but an estimate at the time was 850 tons. The replacement at Peterborough for the run to Kings Cross was New England's new No.4800 (60829), to become one of that shed's hardy annuals over the years.

At Kings Cross, incoming expresses that exceeded the platform length required special regulations to enable them to be dealt with safely. With the longest it is quite possible that the rear of the train was still in Gasworks Tunnel, and Belle Isle was authorised in such circumstances, by prior arrangement, to send an engine in behind it at extreme caution, to handle the excessive train length. All this and air raids too!

The wartime schedule was eased a little, but the principal expresses continued to load to around 20 coaches, and the V2s ran alongside the Pacifics in daily passenger duties. Few records were published of the wartime running, and some were certainly examples of crews either tired or coping with problems. There were on the other hand, some remarkable performances. For example No.4886 (60915) worked a 700 tons express from Newcastle to Grantham, gaining 11¼ minutes on the wartime schedule, and running the 44.15 miles from passing Darlington to stopping at York in 46 minutes. On another occasion

No.4884 (60913) ran 700 tons from Doncaster to Peterborough, 76.6 miles, in just under 90 minutes, her driver carefully observing the wartime speed limit of 60mph. From Grantham to Kings Cross, No.4786 (60815) took 121mins 20secs with 690 tons, while sister engine No.4785 (60814) took 630 tons in the harder opposite direction in 125mins 18secs, 123 minutes net. Then there was the famous episode of Grantham's Driver Skerrit, who was stopped at Retford on the down line and took over an up express in an emergency. He kept the sectional time from Retford to Grantham with No.4851 (60880) running tender first!

POST-WAR

When hostilities ceased, for some years the schedules remained slow and trainloads heavy, while the railways recovered from the six years of overload, constant shortages of material and neglect of vital maintenance. The identity of the locomotive in front mattered little in the running of services. In the years of austerity the railways, now state owned, were restricted in material and investment in order that industry should recover. While new and more powerful Pacifics were being introduced, the schedules were easy, and the V2s continued to hold their own, not only on reliefs, but on the main services. However, when the Pullman services returned, it was quite unusual to see a V2 in charge – indeed it was usually a

sign of a failure elsewhere. The V2s were not unusual choices for the heavier trains, but the group standard tender limited their operation to less than 200 miles, since it was not a good idea to run to the last shovelful of coal in the tender. However, with careful packing of the tender and skilful firing, it was possible to get north of York to Newcastle or south of Peterborough if necessary.

The V2s had been sent to the GC section just before the war along with a few surplus A1s when, in 1938, 70ft turntables were installed at Marylebone and Leicester. They had worked in from both Doncaster and York previously on cross-country and non passenger services, but now the first V2s went to Gorton and Leicester. They were used on the main passenger services as well as fast freight, and the GC men, who had a tradition of fast running and yielded to nobody, made the new engines fly. North of the Chilterns, they had the railway to do it on as well.

After the war, the GC was powered by a mix of A3s off the main line together with a dozen V2s or so. The A3s tended to get more express work, but the sight of a V2 on the Master Cutler or South Yorkshireman was nothing out of the ordinary. Although it was a popular assumption that these were cast-offs from the main line I doubt whether it was in fact. Leicester appeared to maintain their locomotives well despite a somewhat difficult shed layout, and

when an exchange of locomotives occurred, the ex-GC engines seemed to run well.

With nationalisation, in the long term it was unlikely that the GC would prosper at the expense of the former Midland Division of the LMS, and certainly there were long spells of inactivity on the main line south of Woodford. With the arrival of Richard Beeching came a new culture, and it became the career-wise move to look for economies, line and branch closures in the main. As a result there was great pressure from the BRB to seek out cases for closure, and there was certainly a lot of dead wood about. Skilful pruning rather than the sweep of a scythe was what was wanted, but did not happen very often. It was no surprise that in 1957 the LMR should take the GC section over, and that the old GC main line enter its final decline. The Pacifics were retrieved and a squad of V2s remained, later to be dispersed back to the ER and NER or withdrawn.

The pattern of railway operation in the late 1940s and the early 1950s was still very much as the pre-war timetable, less of course the three streamlined trains, with far fewer services than today but with heavy trainloads of 13-15 coaches. The railways continued to run full restaurant facilities, often divided between first and third class (later second class). The descent from restaurant catering to the microwave and trolley service in the last half-century must have

60829 spent most of her working life at New England, as the layers of grime testify. Here she is, recalling the war-time days of grime, on a down express at Red Hall, south of Hatfield, on July 15th 1960.

been a matter of great sadness for lovers of good food, and even the great British hearty breakfast was threatened before wiser counsels prevailed. Of course the former imposed a huge weight penalty on the trainload without the concomitant benefit of extra passengers, which is why the simpler forms of train catering were introduced.

The initial allocation of V2s generally remained the same but within areas there were various transfers. The initial allocation sent 87 engines to the Southern Area comprising the GN and GC Sections, 71 to the NE Area, and only 26 to the Scottish Area. Even allowing for the Area sizes and their workloads, it looked like the same story as usual, the South getting most of the new engines and the Scots having to manage with less and the obsolete. However, there was a war on, to use the favourite phrase of the time, and the traffic flows were disrupted constantly by enemy action, more so in the south. It was asking too much for the hard-pressed Southern Area to eschew the use of new locomotives in favour of despatching them to the north and carrying on with their own worn-out locomotives.

In fact the situation began to be redressed as things eased, and the Scottish Area received a number of transferred V2s from the NE and Southern Areas. There was a small but steady northward flow of V2s over the years. With the cessation of hostilities in 1945, five Doncaster V2s (Nos.4795, 4796, 4798, 4891 and 4898 – BR 60824, 60825, 60827, 60920 and 60927) and three Gateshead V2s (Nos.4859, 4869 and 4890 – BR 60888, 60898 and 60919) moved to strengthen the Scottish fleet. Normally the transfers were within the BR Region, but there were a few substantial changes, such as in 1951 when seven Kings Cross V2s (60813, 60814, 60821, 60823, 60873, 60892 and 60922) were sent to Scotland at St.Margarets, presumably to replace withdrawn locomotives and to provide additional left-hand drive machines. The arrival of COLDSTREAMER was highly appropriate. Strangely, 60814 and 60821 were returned to Kings Cross after 20 months in Scotland, exchanged with 60818 and 60900. One of the mysteries of the steam age was the whole business of transferring and its reasoning: it was not merely a system of passing dud or worn out locomotives on to some unfortunate and less streetwise colleague as commonly supposed. In this case I assume that Kings Cross requested the return of these two, since they were amongst the best of that depot's fleet. It resulted in the unprecedented sight of a 64A shedplate for a week or two in North London, no doubt causing cardiac arrest among the lineside gallery!

The V2s maintained their presence as the East Coast route's major fast freight and parcels power, together with their supporting role on passenger work. Individual locomotives moved between depots on the Regions but there was little movement between Regions. So the events of 1953 came as a major upheaval not only in the life of the Southern Region but a small group of the V2s as well. On April 24th of that year, near Crewkerne, BIBBY LINE suffered a broken crank axle. Working an up Exeter-Waterloo express, it could be reasonably expected that the Merchant Navy was at speed, and it was fortunate that nothing disastrous ensued. The Merchant Navy class was withdrawn and examined, and several similar cases were discovered. The remaining Bulleid Pacifics were withdrawn temporarily, leaving the Southern Region seriously short of motive power, although many of the loads and speeds of the services were well within the scope of smaller – and more economical – classes. A number of locomotives were loaned in mid-May, some seven Britannia Pacifics from the Western and LM Regions, while the Eastern Region supplied six V2s, 60893, 60908, 60916 from New England and 60896, 60917 and 60928 from Doncaster. Two more, 60831 and 60902, were held in reserve at Kings Cross and, in the event, not used. A number of B1s were also loaned from the three ex-LNER Regions for work on the SE Division in Kent. The reverberations on the Southern were almost matched by those on the Eastern Region as far as the V2s were concerned. March had only six V2s but loaned two, 60803 to New England and 60938 to Doncaster, while Kings Cross loaned GREEN ARROW to Woodford and 60909 to Doncaster. I cannot imagine why on earth New England and Doncaster, each with a huge fleet of V2s, should require replacements, especially from depots with much smaller allocations. They probably had more V2s 'stopped' for examination or repair than were sent to the SR. Quite why Kings Cross should complicate the situation even further by sending replacements to Woodford and Doncaster taxes the imagination even more. I suspect that there were one or two uncooperative individuals involved at the time. Within three weeks GREEN ARROW, which had always enjoyed special treatment at Top Shed and was a good performer, was back in her old haunts.

The conservatism of drivers was always evident, and although the Eastern V2s were mechanically related to Bulleid's Pacifics with 6ft 2in coupled wheels, three cylinders and wide fireboxes, in other respects they were obviously different. I would have thought that anyone used to pitting their wits against the eccentricities of unrebuilt Bulleid Pacifics maintained in the London area would have found the V2 an easy challenge but there it is. The V2 of course needed to be driven on full regulator to get the best out of fully expansive working, whereas with an unrebuilt Bulleid Pacific one used full regulator with trepidation, partly because of the tendency to slip, and partly because there was more than a little doubt about the cut-off. With a small tender the V2s were generally kept to the Bournemouth road, and two early failures with 60916 and 60917 did not help. However, when the V2s were extended, and the drivers began to gain confidence in them, speeds up to 90mph could be attained. Salisbury men had a reputation for fast running, and it is a pity that the V2s were not used more on the Exeter road. In later years some the Salisbury men such as Fred Hoare, who drove the A4s on special trains, regarded the A4s as a class apart. One feels that the V2s would have been well liked there. The B1s, which were good, simple, strong and reasonably economical machines, attracted critical views on the SE Division, so one should perhaps keep a grain of salt handy.

POST-WAR WORK BY DEPOT AND AREA

On the main line, Kings Cross kept their dozen or so V2s in good external condition, and during the summer months there would be six-eight V2s running good monthly mileages on express passenger work. It was not unusual to hear of 8,000 miles per month by those in good condition. For example in summer 1954 that elite consisted of Nos.60800, 60814, 60821, 60828, 60855, 60862, 60902, 60903, 60909, 60914, 60943 and 60983. Many of the top link firemen were passed for driving, and it was not unusual to see a familiar face on the other side of the cab for a change, taking a V2 on a relief to Grantham and back. They were competent enginemen, and they knew the road well. For example I remember seeing Jim Wilson, Ted Hailstone's fireman, taking GREEN ARROW to York with the Norseman one Saturday morning.

The V2s were worked hard, and one of the turns on which one would expect a Pacific, the up Flying Scotsman, a heavy train, was occasionally hauled on a Saturday by a Top Shed V2. This was before it became a lodging turn for the A4s, and the V2 was not a last minute substitute but had been rostered for the duty. One of the V2s in good condition – or even someone else's – such as 60821, 60855 or 60876 would be seen heading north and at first one wondered whether it would be replaced for the return trip, but in the afternoon, after the Non-stop and 12.00 from Newcastle had gone south with their A4s, one heard the familiar sound of the quicker V2 bark in the distance. She would roar past, regulator wide open and pulling hard, making a decent speed.

Top Shed appeared to have no duds, but maybe it was simply good maintenance. Possibly they used the same good Rossington coal that fuelled the A4s. One V2 should have been as good as another, but the limitations of the single blastpipe together with the self-cleaning equipment and often lower quality fuel imposed variations in steaming capacity. The Top Shed engines worked long diagrams and there was little opportunity to hide a poor performer. For many years they had the Alpha and Omega, the first V2 GREEN ARROW and the last, No.60983. As mentioned above, apart from three weeks' stay in the country at Woodford as a temporary replacement, GREEN ARROW was always a Top Shed locomotive. For the film 'The Ladykillers' 60814 and 60821, together with ex-works L1 No.67799, were polished and associated with brand new 16 ton mineral wagons, still, if I remember correctly, with white painted tyres. It would have been difficult to think of a less typical freight train. Sunday excursions were part of the railway scene in those days, and for example top link driver Jim Edwards had a pleasant day taking 60821 from Kings Cross to Scarborough and back. 'Nearly as good as a blue'un' was his comment. Unusually for a weekday, on one occasion an ex-works V2, 60855, was turned out for the 10.40 slow and up Flying Scotsman from Grantham, and rolled into Kings Cross 10 mins BT (before time). The driver was a fairly new man in the top link, named W Hoole.

One of the most remarkable events post-war involving a V2 – or rather three V2s – occurred in early summer 1956. Making my way home on a Tuesday evening behind an N2, plodding past Belle Isle, I passed one of Top Shed's hardy annuals, No.60914, about to back down to the terminus. The V2 was immaculate, but what astonished me was that she was carrying the Yorkshire Pullman headboard! I knew that they had occasionally worked it pre-war, but the down train was now a 460 tons load, and a lodging turn to Leeds. Out of every 1000 times, for 999 it was always an A4, at least until the later 1950s when the A3s were redraughted and restored. I had changed trains at Finsbury Park, and sure enough, the V2 came thundering past with the Pullman at Wood Green. Therefore, notwithstanding the feeling that it was a fluke and I was unlikely to see it again, I loaded my camera and took it to work. With a fine sunny evening, I got an earlier train, and having caught a glimpse of a clean V2 in Top Shed yard, lay in wait at New Southgate. My reward was a fine shot of No.60950, another of Top Shed's best, complete with headboard, roaring north with the Pullman. That was not all, for on the Thursday, although the weather was by now dull and wet, Top Shed achieved the hat-trick by turning out another immaculate V2, No.60903. Strangely, these three evening occasions have eluded the hawk-like gaze of the chroniclers of matters ex-LNER. Oh, and yes, they all returned on the 9.50am from Leeds the next day.

It was very unfortunate that the V2s could not have been made compliant with the GE structural requirements. At one time No.60814 was spotted entering Liverpool Street station to test the clearances, but nothing came of it. The reason for prohibiting the V2s from the terminus would have been one of two reasons, assuming that there were adequately long turntables. Either they were too heavy for structures such as Manningtree swing bridge, or they were too large for the structure gauge. The GE track was no great shakes for a heavy locomotive pre-war, and it has required enormous investment to lift the track quality and robustness to its current level. Before the 1939-45 war it was freely described as 'the tramway'. One could understand that. The K3, at RA8, managed it, as did the BR Britannia Pacifics after the war, powerful two cylinder machines, with a heavier hammer blow. Many restrictions were laid down regarding locomotive use, and despite the renewal of structures over time, those restrictions were rarely reviewed. One would have thought that by investing in bridge strengthening or improving clearances, the class could have gained entry to Liverpool Street and galvanised GE express running. Nevertheless, I always felt that the third cylinder was one too many for the GE, and they were happy with their Britannias performing superbly.

March gained a small fleet of up to six V2s (60803, 60830, 60858, 60899, 60938 and 60948 as a rule) for the express service to York plus two lodging turns with freight. It was customary to loan one or two V2s, ironically, to New England at summer weekends. There

Former Top Shed 60821 at Hatfield on August 12th 1961. The V2 has moved to New England in the declining years of steam, as is evident from her external condition.

were a number of fast freight services to and from Whitemoor Yard, avoiding the main line and serving the East London and Anglian ports. York's V2s and B16s were a daily sight at March, while the March V2s went north as far as York and sometimes beyond.

When we come to the large fleet at New England, a vision of dirty and leaking V2s might come to mind. Filthy, of course, very often, but it was a grave mistake to assume that the machine was as neglected as its outward appearance might suggest. Sometimes a scruffy V2 has pulled away with the following driver expecting to run on distants, only to find himself left for dead! However, it must be admitted that more often the reverse was the case. Provided the engine would steam it would always run. The A2s of all sorts lived out years of relative retirement at New England working the few express duties and the stopping services, and as a result the V2s worked on parcels and freight of all sorts. They worked north, again on the fast freight services to the Leeds and NE areas, usually preferred to the Pacifics for the smaller grate and comfortable ride. Many are the tales of New England's V2s coming to the aid of a failed Pacific, while on summer Saturdays they seemed to be powering a significant proportion of the traffic. They nearly always seemed to be working from another depot, and it was fair game for anyone to appropriate one for a relief or excursion. Indeed I sometimes wonder how the New England Shedmaster managed to keep track of his fleet!

The same might easily be said of Doncaster and York's large V2 complements which, though they had extensive freight diagrams, had enough V2s to provide assistance to other depots. When traffic was busy, the southbound West Riding expresses disintegrated into separate trains from Leeds, Bradford and Hull, which brought Doncaster's A3s and V2s into play. Sometimes a V2 or even a B1 from Bradford would come through, but the latter had to be a low mileage one to keep up with the larger engines without delaying.

The small GC fleet of V2s was used throughout from Marylebone to Manchester and into West Yorkshire to York, until the 1500v DC electrification from Manchester to Sheffield and Wath displaced them. Their work was versatile, from express to slower freight and parcels, even stopping services at times. The GC section had no really testing loads requiring sustained high speeds like the main line, but the lighter trains could fly on the easy stretches north of Aylesbury.

The NE Area that became the NE Region of BR had its V2s mainly concentrated on three sheds, at York, Gateshead and Heaton, with one or two V2s at Tweedmouth for piloting duties and the few freight services originating or changing locomotives at Berwick. As the 1950s advanced, V2s were moved to Darlington, Thornaby and the group at Tweedmouth was increased. Their duties varied as elsewhere on the old LNER, mainly fast freight and parcels services together with secondary and special passenger work. Occasionally a V2 would appear on the Queen of Scots in place of one of Neville Hill's A3s, borrowed either from York or Heaton. Otherwise the appearance of a V2 on the principal passenger services was a sign that all was not well somewhere, or else a Pacific had failed up country. The freight turns included cross-country services as well as main line, which took the NE V2s to March, Woodford, Carlisle and Edinburgh.

The Scottish V2s were inevitably associated with the fast fish traffic from Aberdeen and Dundee, although they were used on passenger and general heavy freight. The majority were allocated to St.Margarets, which steadily acquired more as diesel traction started to appear. Haymarket was essentially a Pacific shed, but it had a dozen or so during the war years. Most went elsewhere afterwards, the depot keeping only three or four as reserves, immaculately cleaned. The V2s worked over most of the main lines from Edinburgh to Aberdeen, Perth, Glasgow and Carlisle, and after nationalisation they were used on the ex-LMS routes from Aberdeen to Glasgow and Carlisle, Dundee-Perth, and the main lines in the Edinburgh-Stirling-Glasgow triangle. The famous 15.30 West Coast Postal, a heavy train from Aberdeen to Perth, was regularly worked by the Ferryhill V2s in the last few years of steam, until redundant Pacifics displaced them. The V2 would then run from Perth to Carlisle via Motherwell with the postal section, while another locomotive took the rest of the train to Buchanan Street. The V2 would then work the down service back, a round trip of 480 miles.

The V2s will be remembered for their years of toil on the arduous Waverley route. The depot layout at St.Margaret's was dreadful, awkwardly laid out with the main line on a heavy curve running through the middle of it (Health & Safety at Work Act – where were you?) with trains travelling downgrade from Waverley at moderate speeds. The noises that their V2s made were not at all indicative of assiduous maintenance, perhaps more indicative of minimal attention, and the sound of the exhaust was rarely other than uneven and irregular, memorable if painful. Nevertheless, they slogged over Falahill and Whitrope for two decades, and shifted mountains of freight.

A detailed description of the work of the class is given in the RCTS 'Locomotives of the LNER' Part 6C. Two V2s, one sounding typical and the other sounding more like a low mileage engine, were recorded by the late Peter Handford for his 'Trains in the Night' LP. They were and hopefully still are available, masterly recordings both of the Gresley V2, and of the still of the night. If you have never heard one in daily service, seek this recording out and listen. GREEN ARROW is beautifully preserved, but she doesn't sound like her sisters used to in daily service. The short connecting rods and the less rigorous maintenance of the valve setting due to wear in the motion gave a high mileage V2 an unmistakeably irregular exhaust beat. Some of York and New England's worst were quite distinctly in waltz time, with the return beat of the middle cylinder almost lost completely!

Top right. **The GC main line, at times of major sporting occasions, carried a wide variety of special trains, often with visiting traction from other Regions. This occasioned a stampede of railway photographers to such as Neasden and Wembley. On this occasion, May 19th 1951, the engine on the special was a local V2, 60817, working from Wodford Halse.**

Below. **60844 brings a passenger train into Dundee off the Tay Bridge on August 28th 1965.**

GREEN ARROW, brand new at Kings Cross, on the Scots Goods, the task for which she was conceived and built. Probably a 1936 photograph.

No.3685 (60973) was a Ferryhill V2 by the end of the war, and here she is slogging up the 1 in 70 through North Queensferry on to the Forth Bridge. It was commonplace to find the number cleaned up – during the war the locomotives were so filthy that it was essential to ensure that crews used the correct one. There were occasions when they didn't! Photograph W. Hermiston, www.transporttreasury.co.uk

CHAPTER FIVE
FAST FREIGHT

One of my happiest memories of the steam era on the East Coast main line was to see the V2s moving fast freight. Near London, in the afternoon there was 266 down, the Scots Goods, preceded in earlier years by its first part, 262 down, often 60 vehicles long, followed an hour later by a sister V2 with 714, another lengthy fast freight to York Dringhouses. Three long trains striding north, and in the evening there were the up trains, the fish from Hull, 579 and 581 up, then later, 611 up. Then there were the lesser and slower trains as well such as 1113 up, the Doncaster Goods.

Even better was the sight of the fast freights at Hitchin or further north, V2 after V2 with long trains, flying north at 60-75 mph. In the afternoon, once the afternoon Newcastle with its top link Grantham A1 had cleared, to see the signals clear again, and in the distance the familiar shape of a Green Arrow flying north with a huge train behind. The high point was in the evening, for once the Aberdonian had gone, a procession of fast freights followed. Sometimes one wondered about the stability of the short wheelbase wagons in the trains, but with 60ft jointed track

still yet to be replaced by CWR, hunting was not a problem.

If only the railways could have invested in their fast freight services how different might things have been. We lads saw it, even Dr.Beeching saw it, but sadly, few others outside the industry could see. The fast freights were usually well loaded, and were often heavier than their passenger counterparts. The power required as distinct from drawbar pull was not high of course since power is a product of pull and speed, and even fast freights were not expected to climb Stoke Bank at 60mph! A V2 in reasonable condition could usually run, and down country one could see them flying along with big loads behind.

At Kings Cross the 1A link covered the principal fast freight turns, and they had a group of V2s in first class condition for the diagrams. These were as follows in the mid 1950s:-

268 down, 2.05 Kings Cross Goods to Niddrie (As far as York)
611 up, 21.00 Fish York-Kings Cross Goods.

714 down, 16.15 Kings Cross Goods to York Dringhouses.

273 up, Inverkeithing to Kings Cross Goods (From York)

266 down, 15.10 Kings Cross Goods to Niddrie (As far as York)
555 up, 21.10 Newcastle Forth to Kings Cross Goods (From York)

524 down, 23.30 Kings Cross Goods-York Dringhouses. (To Doncaster)
589 up, 18.55 Fish to Kings Cross Goods (From Doncaster)

611 up was always known as the 'Buckingham Palace Special' since it was reputed to carry the fish that would be bought for the Royal household. It was not heavily laden, was hauled by a Kings Cross V2 in top condition, and the crew were going home. I always found that 'job and finish' was the finest incentive on the railway, and it was certainly true here. 611 up was, apart from the principal passenger services, the fastest thing on wheels on the GN main line. Fish vans were selected and specially maintained, I believe, and were allowed to run at 75mph. That would be the average speed very often! The fish trains were all fast, the advantages being that the guard, who bore the brunt of the physical

Top Shed's No.60821, fresh from Doncaster Works, heads the southbound class C Inverkeithing Goods, 273up, on May 31st 1956. The train is on the up main, just clearing the old intersection bridge north of Sandy carrying the Bedford – Cambridge branch line.

60841 heads an up Class H freight past Red Hall, Hatfield, on April 14th 1962. The New England V2 had been rebuilt with separate cylinder castings in 1959. The driver appears to be using a longish cut-off for some reason. As he has the distant, perhaps the V2 is recovering from a Temporary Speed Restriction (TSR).

discomfort, wanted to get home early as well, and most services ran at night when Authority was elsewhere. The brake vans were usually in good condition, and on some services that attached, such as 581 up picking up the Goole vans at Doncaster, the vans were attached behind the brake. It was said that they were helpful in improving the riding of the brake at speed.

Two or three services were worked by returning Pacifics from Grantham, which ensured fast running, and even the humble B1s returning from Hull were often right up behind the Copley Hill A1 cruising south with the Queen of Scots. There was a story, the truth of which I cannot vouch for, that a top link driver was caught doing 'the ton' with a fish train returning from Grantham. And incidentally, it was before that elite group included the name of Bill Hoole. The Pacific on the 22.35 to Edinburgh, both a sleeper and mail train, was a top link A4 turn, returning from Grantham on the 23.25 freight from Lincoln Holmes, 1355 up. On occasions, with Kings Cross men returning home, that was a very fast freight indeed.

New England had surprisingly few fast freight turns to the south, although their V2s as mentioned before, seemed to participate on behalf of other depots a great deal. They worked a number of trains of lower classification, but they had several diagrams that took them to York and Newcastle. March had one or two

turns to York over the Joint Line via Lincoln, but some GE traffic travelled via New England, forming faster trains northwards.

Doncaster's V2s had at least six fast freight turns to London, three of which were on Hull fish trains, as well as a few parcels services. It was not always easy to track down the Doncaster turns, since on the GN apart from those at Kings Cross, the V2s were not always certain to return as diagrammed; they were freely 'borrowed' between sheds and any GN V2 could turn up on anything.

UP
103 up, class C 5.03 Parcels to Kings Cross
1113 up, class E Bkd 13.45 Doncaster Decoy to East Goods.
579 up, class C 16.09 Fish to Kings Cross Goods (From Hull)
1321 up, class D 21.50 Doncaster Decoy to East Goods.
591 up, class C 23.55 Fish to Kings Cross Goods (From Hull)

DOWN
1016 down, class D 00.05 Kings Cross Goods-Doncaster Decoy.
1116 down, class D 07.35 Clarence Yard-Doncaster Decoy.
812 down, class C ECS 11.15 Kings Cross Goods-Doncaster.
102 down, class C Pcls 19.25 Clarence Yard-York.
122 down, class C Pcls 23.00 Kings Cross-York.

Doncaster's turns were noted with more than usual care since 'Carr Loco' as it was widely known, was not averse to giving a returning overhauled locomotive a spot of running-in. The 19.10 York parcels from Kings Cross was the favourite for many years, though not a heavy or particularly fast service.

Although Doncaster provided men and engines for most freight services, both Ardsley and Copley Hill lobbied for and each won a lodging turn to London on freight. Ardsley already had one involving the 19.35 up parcels service from Wakefield and the 13.18 back, for which they nominally had two A1s, but in fact almost anything was used and it was rarely one of Ardsley's own locomotives. Each depot was provided with three V2s, which were kept in splendid external condition for much of the time. Copley Hill worked the 20.00 from Leeds Goods to East Goods (1343 up) at Finsbury Park, returning on the 19.15 from Kings Cross (1224 down) the day after. Ardsley worked the 22.22 from Leeds Goods (1357 up), returning on the 21.15 (1266 down). The Ardsley service returned at 18.20 on Saturdays while the Copley Hill engine laid over until Monday night. The spare V2s were sometimes used on passenger turns to Grantham or Doncaster. For much of the time the V2s ran like clockwork, and it was unusual for a Pacific to be used. If a V2 was not available, Ardsley often used a B1 4-6-0, especially one of the last built

One of the Top Shed favourites over the years, 60862 with the down Scots Goods, north of Sandy on May 31st 1956.

60875, from Doncaster, with an up freight at Red Hall, south of Hatfield, on May 17th 1952.

with manganese liners. On two occasions they went so far as to use a J39 0-6-0 and even a GNR J6 0-6-0.

The Ardsley turn was accident-prone as I have mentioned several times elsewhere. On Saturdays in the summer, Top Shed would be short of power by midday, and by the evening the Ardsley engine had usually gone north earlier on something else such as the 13.18 Leeds. However, by evening things were easier, and often one might find an unbalanced A3 being returned north. However, on three occasions, whether by mishandling the brake or misreading the signals, the A3 overran the Arlesey bottleneck and plunged into the boggy ground behind Arlesey down platform, setting the breakdown crew a difficult task. The up train fared little better over the years, 60861, on April 9th 1954, overrunning and slithering to a halt in the brambles by Oakleigh Park station beyond the sand drag. Then 60865 through no fault of her driver ran into a pile of wrecked wagons at Hitchin South, bowling over an L1 2-6-4T on the up slow, and finally a collision at Sandy causing the first A1 to be withdrawn. Those are the incidents that I can remember – there were no doubt others.

York worked two freight duties into London, sometimes a third for a period. One, I believe was the 21.30 from Stockton, (551 up), which returned on the 20.15 to Dringhouses in the evening. At different times they worked the first part of the Scots Goods, 262 down, partly consisting of empty meat containers for East Scotland, and the 16.15 to Dringhouses. The up leg of the diagram was an up freight, followed by servicing and then the 9.25 'Parley' from Peterborough. York worked to Sheffield, and down the GC as far as Woodford, as well as east and west, and of course northwards. As time wore on and bridge renewals opened other routes where their RA9 route restriction might have been a problem in earlier times, the class were used on trips across to the LMR.

For a shed that had 30 of the class on its books, York quite often made use of its B16 4-6-0s, nearly always the rebuilt engines, on the V2 freight turns. While they were a smaller engine without the reserve of the big Doncaster boiler, a grate one third smaller on a free-steaming engine no doubt spoke volumes to the man with the shovel. They seemed to cope well and were popular, even if they lacked the muscle of the V2s for the larger and faster trains.

The V2s at Gateshead and Heaton were not often seen south of Peterborough or Grantham, for they were normally limited by tender capacity. On a few occasions, especially when Tyneside engines worked to London more freely, a V2 replaced the rostered Pacific. Andy Robson, who fired Pacifics on the London lodging turns from Gateshead, remembers No.60944 deputising on such an occasion. It must have called not only for a carefully and fully coaled tender, but skilful and economical enginemanship of the highest order. Now and again one was borrowed for a trip to the capital before returning north. They did work holiday and summer relief services to Grantham, as well as parcels and fast freight. Two or three Kings Cross Pacific overnight turns involved returning on fast freight, and the changeover was at Grantham, necessarily. The NE V2s worked down to Whitemoor, Leicester and Woodford Halse with the Newcastle-Poole service and on freight. The latter depot used them for a trip to London, returning with the 15.00 semi-fast service. Otherwise, there was a fairly busy freight service northbound, powered by V2s and K3s, and on a footplate trip one might pass a dozen or so on the other road between Newcastle and Edinburgh. For a long while Tweedmouth had a few V2s for pilot duties, but there were often one or two others in the up yard.

Above. No.60877, once a GC section V2, was at York with nearly a third of the class on May 2nd 1963. Here she is working hard on the down slow with a heavy freight.

60880 with a down fast freight on August 5th 1960, with steam shut off for the south curve at Hatfield. The identity of the train is problematic, as the fast freights hauled by Doncaster V2s were often fish empties or ran earlier in the day, and it is more likely to have been borrowed or used as a replacement for a failed locomotive.

One of the Kylchap V2s, 60902, heads the Inverkeithing goods, 273 up, on the up slow passing Langford Bridge on May 31st 1962. This was the return working of the 16.15 Dringhouses goods, 714 down, which, until the introduction of the Kylchap V2s, had caused considerable operating problems.

New England's black sheep, No.60845, standing at Swindon Works. The V2 is fitted up for testing, with an extended indicator shelter and tarpaulins to protect the testing staff and the footplate occupants from the British climate. The ex-GWR dynamometer car is behind so one presumes that the road testing is in full swing. The V2 had two spells at Swindon, May – September 1952 and November 1952 – May 1953. I would imagine that this picture was taken in the second spell. The two spells were separated by "casual" repairs (an unfortunate description) at Doncaster Works, during which the Swindon community were able to rub their eyes in disbelief.

Woodford's 60831 runs away from Ricksmansworth on February 26th 1956 with a stopping passenger. The V2 has a tremendous blow around the front end, reminiscent of the rebuilt Mikados. The leading coach appears to be the front of a twin-art or quad-art set, and although it looks more like the latter, I cannot remember any on the GC section.

CHAPTER SIX

PERFORMANCE

The V2 was envisaged as a general purpose locomotive, but as it was developed and built it was capable of powering the relief passenger, freight and parcels services, and deputising for a Pacific on the principal passenger trains when required. Except for those services that used routes where RA9 power was prohibited, the V2s swept the board as the all-purpose utility locomotive, and for two decades the faster freight of the LNER and its successor was hauled by the V2s as described above. It was a pity that the V2 did not take part in the 1948 Exchanges since its economy and general ability could have been compared with the West Country and the principal mixed traffic 4-6-0s. My knowledge of the East Coast main line is obviously slanted towards the south, but I cannot recall any instance of a V2 being regularly *diagrammed* for express passenger work on the main line. The March sextet obviously were there partly for the passenger turn to York, and there were other diagrams on the GC which the V2s worked regularly. It is one of those strange features of railway operation that while the V2s often accounted for 15-30% of the main line passenger services, they were always there in place of a Pacific and not diagrammed as such.

However, it had been noticed soon after their introduction that, despite slightly smaller coupled wheels, the V2s could handle most passenger duties. Post-war, despite having no less than 202 Pacifics and a W1, it was surprising how much use was made of the V2s. On busy days before a bank holiday, or on summer Saturdays, they were used in numbers. Given the situation, with extra services to power, V2s off cancelled freights were used together with anything else that could borrowed or otherwise appropriated. I strongly suspect that Shedmasters were reluctant to use their best locomotives on anything that had no fixed balancing duty and preferred to use one from New England, Doncaster or York. Whether true or not, that is certainly how it appeared.

In the steam era, the downtime for a locomotive was far greater than it is now for modern traction, and the number of locomotives needed for say 12 diagrams could run to 18-20 to cover boiler washout, inspections, casual repairs, intermediate or general overhaul, and failures simply awaiting attention. Depots were not awash with fitting staff. So a large depot such as Kings Cross, having provided power for some 30 down expresses on a Saturday morning, would look decidedly empty by lunchtime, apart from the 'stopped' or unserviceable locomotives. Visiting V2s on freight services had been sent north for a return trip, and it was with some desperation that the 9Fs and a B16 4-6-0 were pressed into service. Grantham was probably no better off, and famously returned the engines on their diagrammed turns, with at least one spectacular 9F sprint down Stoke Bank, and a B16 on the up White Rose. On one occasion Peter Townend told me that the cupboard really was bare and he was racking his brains to find an engine to power, I think, the 13.45. The following trains could be covered by locomotives being rushed through servicing. The Shedmaster's guardian angel intervened in the shape of an overlooked V2 that had worked up to Welwyn Garden City with a pigeon special, and had run light to Kings Cross to turn. It was soon under way back north!

Half a century ago, the railway was much less reliable overall. The locomotive's condition and the fireman's shovel were still the crucial variables. The

A long term resident at New England, 60832 (only a solitary electrification flash stands out of the grime) heads an up express past Red Hall signalbox, south of Hatfield on March 4th 1961. The stock is the BR standard non-corridor type used on outer and inner suburban services, rather giving the lie to the express headcode of open lights.

New England's 60842 south of Hatfield with an up relief express on August 15th 1955. The footplate passenger looks suspicious; no legitimate footplateman 'would expect to retain ownership of such a vast cap for long on the footplate!

deterioration in timekeeping was usually, but not always down to a V2, whose fireman had got into trouble with a dirty fire or an engine that just wouldn't steam. As many were fairly filthy, one could only tell when the V2 was on the road and opened out. Then one could get a pleasant surprise. After a fast run from London with an apparently down-at-heel V2, it was a favourite trick at Peterborough for the Kings Cross men to greet their reliefs in fluent Cockney with 'Best o' luck, mate, she's a barstard' and walk off down the platform grinning. I remember New England's 60832 taking over the 22.20 from Kings Cross, a heavy night sleeper, at Grantham instead of an A1, and after a painful passage to York, with a fresh crew she set off for Newcastle in great style, the driver intent on regaining his arrears, oblivious to the general desire to get some sleep! Perhaps he wanted to get home. Digressing, I cannot imagine how regular overnight travellers managed to sleep with the number of engine changes and the predominance of single blast Pacifics on the East Coast route. BR had the cheek to charge members of the public for the privilege of being kept awake too! I can remember occasions when my interest in the operations was at its lowest, for example as a relieving Grantham Pacific bumped into the leading coach buffers with more vim than was appropriate

after midnight. Or worse, at Newcastle. Experience taught that a bottle of the heavier red wine was a very acceptable anaesthetic so long as one took the precaution of telling the steward of one's destination.

The V2s, by common consent, could certainly run fast, and rode smoothly at speed perhaps with the exception of the aftermath of the 1939-45 war. Cecil J. Allen and O.S. Nock were the only two significant commentators on locomotive performance before the 1939-45 war, and both were quick to note that the new V2s of 1936 had soon been put on express passenger duties, and had acquitted themselves with distinction. York's growing squad of V2s had been used to stand pilot and had taken over on the Coronation and West Riding Limited in emergency. The presence of a pony truck had not been a deterrent to high speed, and it was clear that the V2s could be used on work that their predecessors, the K3s, could not. At least not without the probability of the unfortunate crew's shadows falling across the threshold of the unwise Shedmaster's office for a second time!

Bearing in mind the proportion of passenger services worked by V2s, they are however severely underrepresented in the list of published performances. Published performances were a blend of those where the recorder could choose

the service and hence the likely motive power, and those where he could not. Given a choice between a top link Pacific with a keen crew and a run-of-the-mill V2, the preference was obvious. Not many enthusiasts were inclined to spend their money logging a very mundane performance, and as a result the published performances gave a somewhat misleading impression. And of course much of the V2s work was on fast freight and therefore was inaccessible.

Yet a V2 was a Pacific in all but wheel arrangement, and one ought not to find something remarkable about the better performances. Indeed one might wonder why some performances were not so good as they should have been. The V2s occupied a sort of second-class existence, only appearing on express passenger turns in busy periods or as replacements. Some depots were able to reserve better coal for express work as already mentioned, and freight and parcels locomotives had lower quality coal. Self-cleaning equipment badly curbed steaming and hence performance of course, and the task of keeping pressure up with lower quality coal seemed to tax the less experienced firemen. And of course, not every driver was a Hoole, Swan or Hailstone, and simply stuck to his schedule. If the signalmen stopped him, he was certainly not going to thrash his engine, and his mate, in order to retrieve time. In truth, the majority took that view.

Kings Cross depot was slightly different from the others in that most of the work was on express passenger or freight for the bigger locomotives and as has been explained earlier, their V2s were usually well maintained. So they were able to put them on to the out-and-home turns in the summer with confidence. As these turns were usually worked by the second link, which comprised very experienced men who for one reason or another preferred not to lodge, the quality of running was much the same as with the Pacifics. Gateshead, Heaton and Haymarket were in a similar position, although the number of extra summer services were less.

In the steam era, locomotive performance rarely achieved the maximum level of the design, partly because the development of high power inescapably raised coal consumption and lowered economy, and partly because the quality of performances were determined by the crew and ultimately by the fireman's shovel. Footplate work was hard, unsocial, poorly paid and danger was never far away. Moreover, crews had to work with machines that could have been made far easier to work with, which would have been reflected in improved punctuality. That was hardly likely to motivate a poorly trained workforce, and so schedules were often unchallenging and performance normally adequate and seldom better. Only those men who enjoyed fast running and were determined to arrive punctually, despite the operating problems, showed us what East Coast motive power could achieve. This is of course classic hindsight but nevertheless it is sad to remember how much better things might have been. The performance of the V2s was no exception, and while the locomotives would perform better or worse according to condition and handling, just now and again a keen crew would produce a performance which stood head and shoulders above the others, and showed what the V2 could do if pressed.

In compiling a list, comprehensive but not exhaustive, I found a number of runs, with some of my own, but my old friend Brian Bailey has a larger collection of V2 runs which he has made available to me. The list of published runs is given in Appendix C, and the faster runs are in Appendix D. Back in the early 1950s we both suffered an early introduction to the vagaries of post-war East Coast operation. We had endured a dreadful run by BLAIR ATHOL on the White Rose as far as Doncaster, which we felt had plumbed the depths. The Copley Hill crew were in no hurry to get home. On our return, on the 17.15 from Leeds, a very heavy 15 coach train of 560 tons, all that Copley Hill provided was Doncaster's 60872, the name of which was invariably reduced to KOYLI. We soon found that the depths had not been fully plumbed with BLAIR ATHOL! KOYLI's performance was even worse. Later, all became clear, as Willie Yeadon in his Register dealing with the V2s revealed, that within a fortnight or so, KOYLI went into Doncaster Works for a general overhaul. It says much for a locomotive that even in such a relatively decrepit state, it was considered fit for one of the heaviest turns on the main line. Even with this heavy load and a high shopping mileage, although weak on rising gradients, the Grantham men managed a good sprint down Stoke with KOYLI, with a maximum of 86 mph.

It perhaps says something about the nature of services powered by V2s that the running times varied widely over even a short distance such as Peterborough-Grantham. The multitude of schedule variations also demonstrates the extent to which the timetable planners fiddled constantly with timings in the steam era. Two runs stand out in Appendix C. Late in the steam era, a service departed from Newark at 7.27, calling at Grantham and Peterborough. The load was much less than it might have been ten years earlier and, interestingly, the train engine was the same, one of the two BR double blast V2s, No.60817 of New England. The two runs are of a good quality, ahead of any other runs with a comparable load. In Appendix D I have shown some of the

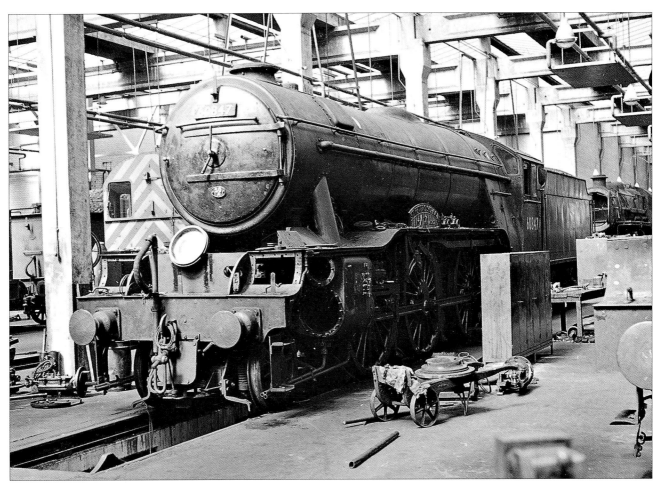

St.PETER'S SCHOOL YORK was quite rightly a York V2 for all but five months of her existence. Here she is under repair in York's new repair shop, built in 1958, which is now part of the NRM. The date is August 17th 1963.

New England's 60850 was said to be the first V2 to be withdrawn, although two NER examples were withdrawn at the same time. Here she is at speed with a down express north of Sandy on July 25th 1959.

60854, then at New England, heads an up 'parley' past Red Hall, Hatfield, on August 15th 1955.

best runs by V2s. There may well be others, especially bearing in mind that by 1950 there were very roughly as many V2s as Pacifics. Also, as I argued earlier, given a choice for an enthusiast between services hauled by top link Pacific or a travel-stained V2, there are no prizes for the answer, and good V2 performances almost certainly went unrecorded.

One of the finest runs behind a V2, indeed behind any steam locomotive between Kings Cross and Grantham was recorded in August 1957 by Brian Bailey. The engine was 60858, borrowed from March, in splendid external condition and still single blast. The train was the 12.10 dep, the first part of the Northumbrian, 13 coaches, 465 tons gross, and normally a Pacific turn. The road was remarkably clear, but as the Queen of Scots was only 10 minutes ahead, there was little opportunity for another train to be slipped in between. The speeds were not remarkable, 80 mph having been achieved twice, but the driver kept his speed as far as possible to 70-75mph for most of the way. The uphill work was outstanding with this big train, 52 at Potters Bar, 58 at Leys and a magnificent 55 at Stoke. Remarkably, there were no signal checks. The train left 5 minutes late, but arrived at Grantham 6 minutes BT on a schedule of 121 minutes. The running time was 109¾ minutes, 107 net. It needs to be remembered that the total

work done on a down run was greater since Grantham was very roughly 250ft above Kings Cross. It was a remarkably fine run with the V2 excellently handled. So many down runs suffered from the fact that the locomotive was due to be replaced at Grantham, and the temptation to leave the new crew to regain late running appealed rather more than an heroic ascent to Stoke.

Appendix D also contains four up runs from Grantham to Kings Cross. The first two were recorded by Brian Bailey, both remarkable performances. The run with GREEN ARROW on the White Rose was notable for the mighty sustained sprint down Stoke Bank with a maximum of 97mph at Essendine. A top speed of 97 mph was the highest published by a V2 to the best of my knowledge, requiring a piston speed similar to an A4 at 105mph. The previous maxima in published runs was 93-94mph, which suggests that Driver Rowe was driving GREEN ARROW hard down the hill, and that the V2 was in splendid mechanical condition. In pre-AWS days fog and signal checks delayed the train at Peterborough, and after a good run, further signal delays made arrival over 12 minutes late. The net times were more than 20 minutes less. The second run with the 17.15 from Leeds was

interrupted at Grantham in order to replace GOLDEN FLEECE, the train heating having failed (in January). The substitute was New England's V2 60828, not long out of Doncaster Works, and she made an excellent run. The speeds down Stoke were not so high as GREEN ARROW, but Driver Walcome had the very unusual experience of running unchecked into Peterborough. With this heavy load the running south of Huntingdon in particular was very good, with a maximum of 82 mph near Little Barford. The train was savaged by signal delays and the TSR for Potters Bar Widening. The actual running time was 7 minutes inside schedule, and the net time was 15 minutes inside.

As I mentioned in Chapter Five, much of the V2 passenger work was on busy weekends, and it was on just such an occasion that I was returning late from York on a Saturday that I too encountered the ability of the V2 to surprise. 'Amaze' would perhaps not be too strong. ROYAL LANCER had come up from York with the first part of the Heart of Midlothian, and after three signal delays costing 8½ minutes, thanks to recovery margins had only lost three minutes by Grantham. I had nine minutes from arriving at Kings Cross on time to departing for home on the 21.54 all stations to Hatfield, a service of *hourly*

Doncaster's 60880 with a heavy up express south of Sandy on March 25th 1953. It looks as though 60880's driver is working her hard. On the up road, this section is where the engine was indeed worked hard, in order to keep up as much speed as possible.

New England's 60905 accelerating past Hornsey with a down relief service on April 16th 1952.

frequency and at the end of a long day, not to be missed if at all possible. I was not at all pleased to see that instead of a Grantham A1, Top Shed's 60943 was backing on for the run to London. Now here was a V2, which despite a well-cleaned exterior, that I knew was due for general overhaul before long having been out of Doncaster Works for a year and a half, and which had been working on parcels and freight for some while.

The signs were far from good, and I was moved to complain to the driver, asking whether he hoped to be on time with this old girl. 'Why?' asked Driver Arrend. The fireman intervened with a comment of considerable warmth that was far from helpful, indicating that such an eventuality was extremely unlikely. When I explained about the connection at Kings Cross, the driver replied that as he lived at Barnet, he too intended, as far as possible, to be on that train! The train was heavy, 460 tons, and as 60943 pulled away up to Stoke, she sounded pretty awful with a ragged beat, making heavy weather of getting away from Grantham. We pounded up the hill with the engine working very hard, still sounding way off-beat. Things were not sounding very encouraging. By Stoke, however, the speed was surprisingly high at 46mph and the passing time at Stoke was good. Down the bank, the V2 was kept hard at it, and the drunken noises from the chimney quickly subsided into a smooth roar, presumably the front end having warmed up, and the speed rose rapidly. The driver was clearly having a go, and

this worn old V2 made the most amazing sprint, averaging 86.6mph from Corby Glen to Helpston and touching 94mph at Essendine. By Tallington we were still doing 91 mph. For all her miles, she must have been in excellent condition mechanically. That this V2 was LNER No.3645, the same one that came to grief a decade or so before with a derailing pony truck at Marshmoor, was not a thought that occurred to me during this prolonged dash down the hill! We ran through Peterborough on the Excursion road, again without a check, and accelerated past Fletton, the V2 now sounding fine. South of Peterborough the quality of the uphill work stood comparison with the best Pacifics on this load, with minima of 61 at Abbots Ripton and 60 at Stevenage. Kings Cross, of course, was not ready for us and we stood, fuming, for seven minutes before being allowed in. The running time was 118¼ minutes, an excellent 107 minutes net. I had been put firmly in my place by Gresley's V2. And yes, we caught the 21.54.

Others had been introduced to the ability of the V2 before. C.J. Allen enjoyed a fast run on the up White Rose from Grantham to Kings Cross, 450 tons and 107¾ minutes including a stop at Peterborough, only to find out at Kings Cross that the locomotive was not a Pacific, but grimy 60950 of New England. This V2 came to Kings Cross and was one of their most consistent performers. Down Stoke the speed was high, but the time from Tallington to stopping at

Peterborough must have been a record, an average of 67.2mph pass to stop! The run to London was steady, the actual time was 5.5.minutes inside schedule, and the net time just over 12 minutes inside. Two other runs are in Appendix D in the form of guards' records, and are described in Chapter 7.

In their early days on the GC the V2s quickly established that they could run fast, and Driver Tetlow of Leicester made as fast a run as was ever recorded on the GC with 4830 (60859) admittedly on a lightweight 255 tons. After delays as far down the line as Princes Risborough, the train was eight minutes late, and the schedule was very tight. After running 19.5 miles at an average of 80.5mph, there was fast running again to the stop at Woodford. The following 34 miles to Leicester were timed at 34 minutes start to stop, but with 90 at Braunston and 88 at Ashby Magna, Driver Tetlow stopped at Leicester in 30mins 9 secs.

The centre of gravity of the railway enthusiast world lay to the south, and fewer examples of good running farther north were available generally. That, coupled with the less frequent use of V2s on the principal services, meant that not many instances of V2 running in the NE got into print. With the impending withdrawal of steam, more attention was given to the Scottish Region and its locomotives. Although the alignment of the routes was often tortuous and the condition of the track in the early 20th century poor, as the system recovered after 1945, the maintenance of the Scottish main lines improved considerably. I remember how Scottish engineers came to the annual permanent way conferences armed with well-nigh perfect traces of track geometry, shaming those of us in the south into a decline. Outside the Central Lowlands, in pastoral Scotland, excellent and conscientious manpower could be recruited, and the track, albeit lightly used, was usually good and often excellent. Despite, I believe, a maximum speed limit of 75mph, drivers would let a smooth running engine have her head, and the long descent from Carmont down to Kinnaber was the scene of some very fast running with V2s, over 90mph on occasion. It was here that BLUE PETER achieved 100mph, or something very close, with the up Aberdonian. On the Caledonian main line, on from Kinnaber to Perth, there were some very inviting stretches across Strathmore, the climax being the dip across the Tay at Luncarty.

60908 with an up express at Red Hall on May 17th 1952. The first coach is an interesting vehicle in a fairly motley collection that emphatically says 'relief'!

Below. **60914 was still a Top Shed V2 when this photograph was taken north of Sandy on July 25th 1959, as will be obvious from the locomotive's condition.**

The up Scarborough Flyer pulls away from Doncaster on August 24th 1957. 60814 is working the Saturday return leg of the York lodging turn.

The second V2 to arrive in Scotland, 60816 spent a lot of her time allocated to Haymarket. It is as a Haymarket engine on July 29th 1954 that she is working a semi fast service that probably started from the short platforms on the south side of Waverley station, crossing from the down Glasgow to the down Fife line in Princes Street Gardens. Photograph Peter Groom.

CHAPTER SEVEN
V2s TO THE RESCUE

I have referred earlier to the occasions when the new V2s were pressed into action, replacing A4s on the streamliners. This became a feature of operating life on the East Coast main lines. Not only did V2s replace Pacifics on diagrams, but as they were usually main line pilots, they were usually the replacements. However, if the pilot had already been used and another had not been prepared in its place, there was often another V2 on shed that could be pressed into service. As an example of East Coast operation, I have quoted two months in the summer of 1954, when there were no less than 15 failures by A4s on the Kings Cross lodging turns, 10 on the road, as right.

In five cases the A4 was unfit to return, possibly due to a hot axlebox or injectors malfunctioning, so it could not be

DATE	ENGINE	DN/UP	TRAIN	LOCATION	RELIEF
1/7/54	60008	D	16.45 TTP	At Newcastle	60150
2/7/54	60014	D	16.45 TTP	Grantham	60853
4/7/54	60015	U	13.50 Leeds	At Leeds	60106
7/7/54	60013	U	14.00 TTP	Hitchin	61097
18/7/54	60006	D	16.45 SuO	At Newcastle	60018
22/7/54	60021	D	16.45 TTP	At Newcastle	60018
24/7/54	60032	D	9.30 nonstop	Hitchin	61075 then 60121
3/8/54	60025	U	13.50 Leeds	Doncaster	60930
3/8/54	60024	U	16.15 nonstop	Doncaster	60048
14/8/54	60029	D	18.00 SuO	Peterborough	60974
16/8/54	60017	U	17.12 exNC	Doncaster	61212
25/8/54	60032	D	9.30 nonstop	Grantham	60113
26/8/54	60029	U	17.12 ex NC	At Newcastle	60002
30/8/54	60025	U	14.00 TTP	Peterborough	60852

No.60825 stands at Waverley on July 17th 1953 with a down service. We may, I think, dismiss the possibility of the headcode being correct: the stock suggests that it would be a stopping passenger service out to Fife. Photograph J. Robertson, www.transporttreasury.co.uk

counted as a failure operationally. On 3 August 1954 it was a busy day at Doncaster, for the pilot, 60930, had gone south having relieved FALCON with the return working of the Yorkshire Pullman the night before. Two and a half hours later sister A4 KINGFISHER failed with a hot axlebox on the Elizabethan and a good A3, DONCASTER, was the substitute for a hard run up to London. SILVER FOX must have failed to the south of Doncaster since a 'Retford Pacific', 61212 was the substitute.

The replacement of GANNET by GREAT NORTHERN on the Elizabethan on August 25th due to the former's hot driving axlebox must have been an interesting sight and experience, and it was a pity no log of the running has surfaced since. A month previously GANNET had failed at Hitchin with the same train with a broken spring hanger on the tender. The train went forward with a B1, 61075 and an A1, SILURIAN took over from Grantham (I think). This was the occasion when she ran through

Newly built V2 4798 (60827) heads an up express through the old station at Potters Bar. When built she went to New England, but later moved to Gorton, then Doncaster, but at her first overhaul in July 1939 the allocation would have been painted on the buffer beam in line with LNER policy. I would guess that the date is 1938. The V2 was one of a number moved to Scotland immediately after the end of the 1939-45 war. Photograph www.transporttreasury.co.uk

to Edinburgh, and returned through to Kings Cross on the Sunday, arriving ten minutes early with Driver Hoole in charge.

V2s stood as pilots very often, although obviously if a Pacific was in suitable condition that was preferred. Many times a V2 has been rushed to the aid of a crew whose locomotive has failed. At Peterborough the pilots were V2s due to the smaller turntable there, and the presence of a New England V2 usually implied a failure in the vicinity. The majority of failures on the road tended to fall into two groups, overheating axleboxes or the legendary middle big end, and fitful or failed injectors. A well known run which was a good example of canny enginemanship was in 1958 when Bill Hoole was driving GREAT CENTRAL on the Flying Scotsman. Unusually, especially for this A1 which was a favourite at Top Shed, the steaming was not good and had deteriorated badly before Hitchin, by which time the injectors were flying off.

To anyone unfamiliar with steam locomotive operation on the footplate, running at speed with more than at least half a ton of white hot fire heating a large pressure vessel at 250psi, in which the water level has fallen and the means of replenishment has failed, is a certain cure for constipation! Bill had given the whistle code at Tempsford – three crows, meaning 'My engine is disabled and I

require a fresh one' in the dry language of the BR Whistle Code Instructions. GREAT CENTRAL had enough life (and water) left, and Bill pressed on at speed, running in to Peterborough 10 minutes early, which gave him plenty of time to take over New England's 60869 and still depart two minutes early. In such circumstances, the pilot crew had plenty of time to rouse 60869 from her morning slumber and get her into shape before transferring to the A1 to drop her fire. 60869 topped Stoke bank at 58mph, which with 374 tons was good going, starting from cold. By setting a good pace, helped by recovery margins, they reached Newcastle four minutes early.

The assumption that a V2 was always standing by, ready to take over and run well, was unwise. For example, on one occasion, on July 2nd 1954, Ted Hailstone was all set to give a command performance on the down Tees-Tyne Pullman with SILVER LINK for the benefit of O.S. Nock who was riding with him. Having gone like the wind, an heroic ascent of Stoke bank was all too much for the prototype, and she came off at Grantham with a hot axlebox. The replacement was 60853, strangely all that Grantham (with 10-11 A1s plus A3s) had to hand. She had a high mileage and was about to go to Doncaster Works. Suffice it to say that Ted had to hammer the V2 to get any speed out of her, but they made a fair run in the circumstances. Ted

told me that the compensation for a really rough old Green Arrow was to see his footplate passenger at Darlington making his way very unsteadily back to the train to clean up. Curiously, on August 18th 1955 exactly the same thing happened with 60853 coming to the aid of SILVER LINK once again, although I believe it was a happier occasion.

Bill Hoole pressed his engines hard in his determination to run punctually or early. The operators of the East Coast main line gave him every opportunity to exercise his skill with frequent delays and checks. In 1953 one of his first trips on the Non-stop, on July 31st 1953, GOLDEN PLOVER failed at Doncaster and MERRY HAMPTON took over, running into Kings Cross a minute early. I remember the A3 vividly, hurtling through Wood Green at well over the permitted speed. Over four years later, on October 12th 1957 Bill was returning from Newcastle on the 8.00 with MALLARD hauling 390 tons. All went punctually and well until the A4 was checked at Moss, following which she came off at Doncaster for an unknown reason. The pilot, Doncaster's V2 60946, set off 10 minutes late, and after a very fast run, got into Kings Cross no less than seven minutes early. The V2 had two TSRs and a slight signal check before Grantham. The schedule was not demanding, 170 minutes from passing Doncaster to Kings Cross, but the running time was 152 minutes gross and 145 minutes net. This was one of the finest performances by a V2, but it was bettered by a sister Doncaster V2 just over ten months later.

On this occasion it was the up Elizabethan, no less, hauled by WILLIAM WHITELAW on August 29th 1958, with a load of 375 tons. Bill Hoole had relieved Driver Redpath of Haymarket and passed into the Eastern Region at Shaftholme Junction RT (right time). But then another unknown calamity overtook the A4 and she came off at Doncaster. Another Doncaster V2, 60852, was pilot, and she took over, restarting the train eight minutes late. The V2 must have been travelling very fast, picking up nine minutes between Grantham and Hitchin, and although badly checked at the old Potters Bar station where she was actually two minutes before time, she ran in on time. The schedule was 151 minutes from passing Doncaster to Kings Cross, and the running time 143 minutes gross. The net time is hard to estimate since guards rarely showed time gained by the locomotive other than in reducing lateness, and if a check and time regained balanced out it was not recorded. With signals at Retford North and Potters Bar,

138-139 minutes net seems a reasonable estimate, an astonishing effort. No doubt both V2s were driven very hard. It is a great pity that neither run was properly timed, at least so far as we know.

While these runs were outstanding, the usual experience was less exciting, if the passing and arrival times, when known, were anything to go by. Whether standing pilot was regarded as a sinecure or not, sometimes the crew of a failed Pacific were given a run down substitute like that for SILVER LINK referred to above. Then it was very much a matter of getting on as well as possible, having to liven the fire, raise pressure, and force as much power as possible out of the locomotive, almost invariably a V2. A canny driver in such circumstances might fail a poor substitute in the knowledge of a better one at the next major station.

Another extra passenger train pounds up Holloway Bank behind yet another New England V2. This is in the days when there were 'excursions', usually on a Sunday morning, such as this one to the Lincolnshire bulb fields. No.60829, bearing her STN number 302, looks to be going well, with her fireman taking it easy for the moment. I would put the period at 1952-53. Photograph A.R. Carpenter, www.transporttreasury.co.uk

No.60848 was another of the few V2s which moved from Scotland to the North East. I suspect the now Gateshead V2 is not long out of Darlington Works. She has a heavy down train, probably one of the principal services, at Beningbrough in summer 1957.

No.862 was a New England engine at this time, and is on an up semi-fast service approaching Hadley Wood station, possibly the 'Mark Lane Flyer', the 7.30 from Nottingham.

After the 1939-45 war, holidays were much more sharply focussed than today and at Easter for example, a handful of extra services were provided around the weekend except on Maundy Thursday, when a vast number of extra services were operated. The summer weekends included many extra services, rising to a climax towards the end of July. Again, at Christmas extra parcels and mail trains were introduced two weeks beforehand, but Christmas Eve was a similar operating climax to Maundy Thursday. Members of the 'GN Mafia' would gather at the lineside or in signalboxes to watch the unfolding events, whether they were dramas or farce. Brian Bailey and I often went to Grantham, an important point in the operations on the GN. When we returned – when – it was possible to compare our notes with our colleagues to what had happened.

Memories of Maundy Thursdays and such like had a common thread: everything ran reasonably well until the afternoon, following which there was a remorseless descent into chaos with many trains running very late indeed. The large fleets of V2s at New England and Doncaster were plundered in order to power the extra trains, and even some of the half dozen at March were borrowed. The latter were usually in fairly good condition. The rush also demanded extra crews, some of whom were less experienced. This large number of extra trains brought Green Arrows out in force, a number of them displaced from cancelled freight services, and in truth a number that were about to join the queue for overhaul at Doncaster or Darlington, and so far from ideal power for expresses. There were often those that were not steaming well, courtesy the self-cleaning apparatus, and they could hold the main line operation to ransom. I can remember the occasional lull on the up main at Cadwell on a summer Saturday afternoon, and eventually the culprit, nearly always a down-at-heel V2 emitting clouds of black smoke, would appear, slogging away at 40-50mph with following expresses block on block behind.

I have included three lists in Appendix E. In the first, two examples within the

Another of New England's long-term residents, 60874, with an up express at Potters Bar in, it is said, late 1959. The fireman leans out of the cab, hoping that he's put the last round on the fire for the twelve mile drop down into Kings Cross. The location, in the shadow of the rebuilt Mutton Lane overbridge, still has jointed track and a recently-quadrupled look about it. A curiosity; indeed two curiosities (for the sight of a clean New England V2 was an uncommon pleasure) was the old BR totem on a V2 turned out in lined black fully two years after it had been superseded. However, the section from Potters Bar station back to the site of the old Mimms Hall signalbox was opened on a temporary basis before the full quadrupling, and I wonder in fact if it is late summer 1957 when 60874 had been given a heavy intermediate overhaul. Insofar as the ATC is concerned a number of Southern Area engines were so fitted for the trial New Barnet-Huntingdon prior to the adoption of AWS as the BR standard. Photograph P. Ransome-Wallis.

Gateshead's 60883 has started away from Newcastle with an up express on May 9th 1954. This photograph pre-dates the Newcastle resignalling which included layout alteration. The signalling then in existence at Newcastle, still maintaining the necessary principles, called for some imaginative interlocking. The proximity of the down train on the left, which must have crossed immediately in front of 60883's train, would normally have required protection in the form of trap points, but there was no room. Presumably it had stopped, but there is no trapping evident to prevent the down train setting back into the up train's path: of course it shouldn't but things like sticking on dead centre occasionally happened. It would be interesting to find out how an apparently unsafe movement was prevented; possibly it was through the interlocking of the signalbox frame. Photograph J. Robertson, www.transporttreasury.co.uk

same week are shown of main line operation at busy times. The first of the two was a record made of the services and locomotives on Saturday July 30th 1955, just about the busiest weekend of the year. The 141 trains, excluding the inner, outer suburban and Cambridge trains and the few loose-coupled WD and 9F trains are set out with times and descriptions. The times are not accurate, since firstly I normally referred to trains by their Working Timetable (WTT) numbers and secondly the operators could not resist tinkering with the running times and they always seemed to change by a minute or two. It was done so as to try to anticipate where major engineering works were planned, but how much would have been saved by sticking nevertheless to one set of running times I dread to think. Certainly it would not have made punctuality better or worse and it might have enabled the timetables to be available, sometimes before the trains started running.

V2s worked 26% of the down and 28% of the up trains. One can see that, like a hand of cards, the Shedmasters had gradually played their trump cards as the morning wore on, and by midday the visiting freight engines for returning services on Monday were being roused from their weekend stupor and pressed into action. One can see from the V2s used that even Copley Hill's 60865 was jolted into use for a return trip to Grantham. The only points of operational interest concerned the Pacifics: GUY MANNERING was on the Gateshead lodging turn instead of one of the roller-bearing twins, and NIGHT HAWK and TEHRAN were borrowed by New England and Grantham

respectively. EMPIRE OF INDIA had been unfit to work the Thursday 9.30 Elizabethan from Kings Cross and LORD FARINGDON had replaced her. Haymarket, having returned the London engine overnight, sent MERLIN up on the Friday. LORD FARINGDON meanwhile had gone to Newcastle with the Tees-Tyne Pullman and returned on the 17.12 on Saturday. The Non-stop A4s resumed on Saturday, and MERLIN was sent home on the 9.40 Newcastle. On that day we had the occasional West Riding B1, including Bradford's 61031 REEDBUCK on a relief, while the two Immingham B1s, 61318 and 61374, were the engines that had been used on the Birmingham turn when new, for very long spells, causing them to join CICERO and SIR VISTO inscribed on the lineside fencing wish list! However, I am supposed to be writing about the V2s!

The second of the two is of the following Friday, August 5th 1955, when again the V2s worked 25% of the main line duties. The only noteworthy visitor was one of the M&GN Ivatt 'Black Pigs' from New England, with a special freight. These were very unusual visitors to the capital. Both days are shown together for comparison. The third record was taken before the Christmas holiday on December 15th 1954 when, once again, lineside sidings were ransacked for stock forming relief passenger and parcels trains. Looking back at the relief services, how did BR have the effrontery to charge good money for elderly coaches, often dirty and fusty through lack of use – and cleaning – hauled by indifferent traction?

The record shows not only the locomotives used at the southern end, but also north of Grantham as well. 'PE' indicates where the locomotives were

changed at Peterborough instead of Grantham. Numbers in brackets indicate where the appropriate locomotive was assumed to have worked the train. The record was an aggregate of several people's recordings. The V2s had again about 20-25% of the traffic, but once again it is the Pacifics that take the attention. The highlight of the day was the new diesel railcar set that left Grantham bound for Boston. Comprising two pairs, it had the jumpers wrongly connected between the sets so that the leading one was running northwards while its mate was in reverse. Advice from teenage observers was ignored, and we watched the set crawl off north with sparks flying from the rear set. Apparently it sat down and died near Peascliffe and shut the shop up for an hour or two while the 'Hammer and Spanner gang' worked out what to do with it! Needless to say the down main was at a standstill well back to Essendine.

Unusually neither of the roller-bearing twins were on the Gateshead lodging turn, but their replacement was not another A1, but even more unusually, SILVER KING worked the turn on Thursday. Still more unusually, the up train arrived behind V2 60875, in her third week at New England having been moved from Doncaster where she had been since building, having replaced a failed Gateshead engine. This must have been one of the few occasions that a V2 worked this duty. Gateshead reacted quickly, replacing WOODCOCK on the up Tees-Tyne Pullman with GOLDEN EAGLE in order to work the 22.15 Night Scotsman back. Knowing her reputation at the time (found to be a leaking smokebox joint) it must have required a strong sense of humour on the part of the Gateshead crew! I am unaware how WOODCOCK was returned. HERRINGBONE with the 8.20 York also failed on that day at Hatfield, and the No.2 link crew had to revisit their earlier years' experiences since all that was available was N2 No.69582 as far as Hitchin, where at least a B1, No.61094, was available. I was sorry not to see it myself, especially the N2.

On all three occasions, the punctuality was not out of the ordinary, at least until later in the afternoon in the first two. The blighted 'Flying Greenhouse' referred to above reduced the down main line to a shambles by about 15.30 in the third case. Trains were usually within five minutes of 'Time', but at busy periods the punctuality gradually faded. Later on, the ability of Kings Cross to clear its four principal arrival platforms promptly whilst despatching extra down services began to tell. Up expresses formed a queue, gradually creeping out to Finsbury Park in such circumstances. It was not helped by a number of troop specials, mainly V2 hauled. These were the days, as mentioned earlier, when our armed services were far more numerous; in 1955 they were further inflated by national servicemen, and most journeys, by far, to and from camp were usually by rail.

The fourth record was the result of a challenge, that I could work a night shift as a signalman. I must admit to a curiosity about what went on overnight, but I think the signalman doubted whether I could stay awake! The record was again supplemented both before and after by friends, as I certainly did not work a 16 hour shift. The date was July 16-17th 1954.

I include it to give a complete picture of the operation of the East Coast main line at night, albeit a quiet one. Now if public libraries held copies of the Working Timetable (WTT), especially the freight WTT, it would be held in the Fiction section. That a freight service was in the WTT was no guarantee that it would run. One can see the sense, since if enough traffic was on hand for one of two services, the first would run and the second not. Unlike advertised passenger services that had to run (in those days), freight services did not. Locomotive diagramming tended to be much more ad hoc as a result.

Unfortunately, as this was almost at the busiest time of year for passenger services, freight activity was at its lowest and there were quite a number of freight cancellations, especially of the slower services. One tended to take little notice of the procession of WDs barking north with loads of empties, or creeping south with smoking brake blocks and a load of coal behind, but there were a dozen movements of freight or light engines in both directions that simply did not run. The consumption of town gas required the railways to haul enormous amounts of coal to the capital in unbraked wagons of great antiquity in many cases, and the corollary was the enormous traffic northwards in empty wagons. When I say unbraked, that means no continuous vacuum brake: all rail vehicles had a hand brake. (Whether it was fully effective was another matter!) By July, with gas production and domestic coal consumption at a low, so too was the coal traffic.

Once again it was interesting operationally. Things ran normally on the down, with the heavy freights all hauled by V2s. On the up road things ran quietly until the locomotive hauling the heavy 17.15 from Leeds failed near Hitchin, and MADOQUA had to stagger the last few miles of Stevenage Bank with some 550 tons. The two Immingham K3s rattled up with their loads of fish, and as the morning empties were cancelled the second, the prototype, returned in place of a V2. I thought of the legions of lineside enthusiasts that would have swooned at the sight of Haymarket's AULD REEKIE, fresh from Doncaster Works, on the Doncaster Decoy goods, 1321 up. Unusually a number of B1s were about, one on 255 up fish, and strangely, another on 611 up, the 'Buckingham Palace Special'. This should have been one of Top Shed's better V2s, and the odd feature was that it was a Top Shed B1. It was unlikely that the B1 would have been sent to York on the lodging turn, and the more likely explanation is that the V2 had been replaced in the vicinity of Hitchin. Another, 61138, came up with an overnight Newcastle express. A number of special trains, possibly troop movements, brought more V2s into London, no doubt heartily appreciated by the Kings Cross Shedmaster, for use later on. Unusually, Gateshead's SIR CHARLES NEWTON was on the lodging turn. The V2s had about 20% of the traffic, reliefs and fast freight, and unusually, the B1s 15%.

60857 approaching New Southgate with a down train. Photograph A.G. Forsyth, Initial Photographics.

GREEN ARROW at Darlington on November 9th 1958. Photograph Brian Hilton, Paul Chancellor Collection.

GREEN ARROW at Top Shed in 1962. Photograph Canon Alec George, www.transporttreasury.co.uk

CHAPTER NINE

V2 PORTFOLIO

GREEN ARROW at Kings Cross shed on May 13th 1956.

GREEN ARROW at York on August 4th 1956. The Kings Cross V2 is quite probably on one of the lodging turns. Photograph A.G. Ellis, www.transporttreasury.co.uk

GREEN ARROW in the familiar surroundings of Grantham Depot yard on August 27th 1958. The V2 is probably on passenger duty waiting to return south, although one or two parcels and freight trains changed engines here as part of a passenger diagram. Photograph Peter Groom.

No.60801 on shed at Tweedmouth on June 3rd 1956. Photograph J. Robertson, www.transporttreasury.co.uk

The third V2, 60802 at Haymarket on May 29th 1960. Photograph J. Robertson, www.transporttreasury.co.uk

A superb portrait of a Gresley V2 on the work they were designed for. Tweedmouth's 60805 climbs north of Grantshouse towards Penmanshiel with a heavy fast freight on September 1st 1956. Photograph J. Robertson, www.transporttreasury.co.uk

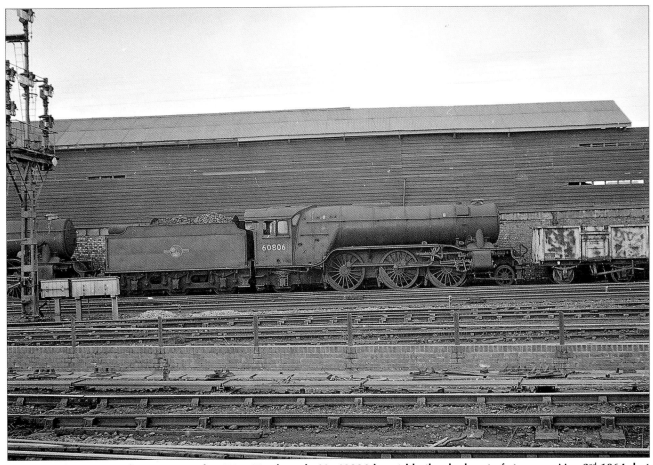

In the last few years, a few V2s moved to West Hartlepool. No.60806 is outside the shed, out of steam on May 2nd 1964, but she was moved to Darlington later in the year.

60806, from Heaton, waits at Craigentinny, Edinburgh with NEIL GOW behind. The absence of the ferret & dartboard totem sets the date at 1948-9 when there was a shortage of transfers at Doncaster. Photograph W. Hermiston, www.transporttreasury.co.uk

No.60807 at Haymarket, immaculate in the BR black livery after a repaint in 1948. Photograph W. Hermiston, www.transporttreasury.co.uk

No.60808 at Tweedmouth, resplendent in dark green livery and with separate cylinders, on June 1st 1957. Photograph J. Robertson, www.transporttreasury.co.uk

No.60809 THE SNAPPER fresh from overhaul at Darlington on November 9th 1958. Photograph Paul Chancellor Collection.

THE SNAPPER at York on 17th August 1963.

The nameplate of No.60809, one bolt missing. Photograph www.transporttreasury.co.uk

No.4780 THE SNAPPER (60809) with a down express on the Fife line passing the entrance to Haymarket shed. There is nothing that specifically identifies the photograph as pre-war or post-war as the V2 is too grubby to be sure. I would plump for 1939 as the date. Photograph W. Hermiston, www.transporttreasury.co.uk

No.60809 THE SNAPPER with an up class E fast freight at New Hailes, near Edinburgh on May 19th 1956. Photograph J. Robertson, www.transporttreasury.co.uk

Heaton's No.60810 with a northbound freight at an unknown location. The fireman appears to have come from a mining family. Photograph Peter Rose.

No.60810 of Heaton is about to come off an up express, to judge by the single headlamp, at Doncaster in September 1953; the V2 is unlikely to be coming on. Expresses from the NE Region only rarely changed engines at Doncaster, and unless the V2 has been failed, it is more likely to have been borrowed. Photograph A.W. Battson, www.transporttreasury.co.uk

Heaton's 60811 stands at Haymarket next to a well cleaned SALMON TROUT. The step-sided tenders had by October 14th 1951 migrated all over the class. If the locomotive took longer to repair than the tender, or boiler, then they would used on another locomotive. Photograph W. Hermiston, www.transporttreasury.co.uk

No.60813 at Tay Bridge on August 16th 1966, showing clearly the unique single deflector. Photographs Paul Cotterell.

No.60813 at Carlisle Kingmoor on August 10th 1965. Photograph Peter Groom.

No.60815 was a Southern Area engine that spent eight years on the GC main line at the end of its life. Here she is at Annesley, the GC shed at Nottingham, on August 30th 1958. From her condition and probable mileage, she had been working freight.

LNER No.4787 (60816) I think at Haymarket before the war. It may be after, but only 883 was turned out in apple green post-war. A number of the V2s working north of Edinburgh had a hole cut in the cabside for a single line tablet catcher, but here is one with the apparatus in place. It was necessary for the Usan-Montrose single line section. Photograph W. Hermiston, www.transporttreasury.co.uk

No.60817 during her spell on the GC, at Annesley, north of Nottingham, in 1955. Photograph www.transporttreasury.co.uk

A sad sight at Tweedmouth as St. Margarets V2 60818 wheezes on her way south with an up fast freight. Perhaps John Robertson caught the train restarting, but there certainly seems to be a bad blow in the middle engine. St. Margarets had a large fleet of Gresley engines, especially the V2s, and from the noise and lack of cleanliness, clearly had trouble most of the time in keeping them in good condition. As the 1960s decline set in things simply got worse. It is difficult to see whether the V2 has AWS but there is no sign on the footplating of the cable conduit back to the cab, which suggests that the date is much earlier than the 1960s rundown. The age of the track and signalling would confirm that it is probably 1953-56. Photograph J. Robertson, www.transporttreasury.co.uk

Both photographs. Dundee's 60818 pauses at Thornton Junction on August 28th 1965 with a stopping service. 60818 was an old Top Shed V2 and one of the last to be withdrawn.

St. Margarets V2 No.60818 at some time between the fitting of AWS by May 1959 and transfer to Dundee in late 1963. Photograph B.K.B. Green, Initial Photographics.

One of Top Shed's excellent V2s of the time heads the up Flying Scotsman southwards from Stoke complete with headboard on Monday, September 19th 1955. The train is one of the Elizabethan sets, appropriately strengthened. According to my ancient notes, the driver was Ted Hailstone. His A4, SILVER LINK, was on the up Tees-Tyne Pullman that day but the famous partnership resumed two days later. As the train was 40 mins late, the regulator would have been wide open, and No.60821 will have been accelerating rapidly downhill! An opportunity for fast running like that was not to be passed by! Three weeks later the V2 went to Doncaster Works for a general overhaul. Photograph Peter Groom.

No.60821 at Top Shed with LORD FARINGDON behind. The V2 looks to be out of steam, and the picture is probably posed. The period is 1953-1956. Photograph E.D. Bruton.

60821at New England, 31st March 1963.

No.60821, freshly returned to Kings Cross from Scotland and an unclassified repair at Doncaster, pulls away from Oakleigh Park with a class K stopping freight on February 28th 1953. This is almost certainly 1111 up, a stopping freight service that was often used for either running in, or retrieving previously failed locomotives from down country. The train was timed, if one can use the verb loosely, to depart Hitchin at 8.25 and normally a New England WD, having worked up to Hitchin, took the train forward to Ferme Park (SX) or Hatfield (SO). 1111 was allowed to take ten hours to cover the 27 miles from Hitchin to Ferme Park, which was in itself a comment on the way railway traffic was handled half a century ago. The train was scheduled so as to call at every siding on the up slow between there and Ferme Park to set down or pick up and having set back inside to conduct business, it had to remain there until a suitable path presented itself for progress further south. The times allowed at the eight calling points varied from a brisk nine minutes at Barnet to over two hours shunting Weetabix at Welwyn Garden City. How this was calculated depended on the traffic offering; it must have been a mixture of experience and a reading of the tea leaves! In reality the schedule was rarely observed and by New Southgate the train would be running about 5-6 hours earlier than its booked time of 17.00-17.45. Photograph R. Wilson, www.transporttreasury.co.uk

Ferryhill's third V2, 60822, moved to Tay Bridge in late 1950. Here she is at Haymarket on June 30th 1957, just back from a general overhaul at Darlington Photograph J. Robertson, www.transporttreasury.co.uk

60824 was a GN V2, and was one of the first batch to be sent to Scotland where she remained for the rest of her working life. Here she is in York shed on May 1st 1966, a long way south for a St. Margarets V2, unless she had paid a visit to Darlington Works, unrecorded in *Yeadon's Register*.

One of the post-war emigrants north of the border, 60825 is stored dead at Seafield, near Edinburgh on August 4th 1962. She was later overhauled at Darlington. Photograph Peter Groom.

St.Margarets V2 60825 pulls away from Dundee station with an up fish train on August 12th 1960. The V2 had acquired a stepped tender early in her life. Photograph Peter Groom.

A rousing shot, despite the rain. 60828, a GN émigré at York, heads the 05.10 Dringhouses-Cardiff Class C freight through Rugby Central on the GC main line, on January 28th 1965. Photograph Jack Hodgkinson.

The archetypical New England V2. No.60828 heads the 14.50 relief north of Copenhagen Tunnel on September 29th 1953. The V2, despite its dreadful appearance, seems to be going quite well with only a slight blow in the left-hand cylinder gland, and the pressure seems to be fine. So perhaps the 14.50 had a decent run to Peterborough. Three weeks later, the V2 went to Doncaster for general overhaul, and nine months after that was transferred to Kings Cross. Photograph A.R. Carpenter, www.transporttreasury.co.uk

New England's No.60829, unusually, is heading the down Heart of Midlothian in place of the usual Heaton Pacific. This was the V2, when new, that hauled the heaviest passenger train on record in the UK. She is at Saltersford, south of Grantham, just recovering from a TSR, with the fireman hard at work by the look of the exhaust. I would guess that it was a late substitution, otherwise a Pacific would have been used. Photograph Peter Groom.

No.60830 at her home shed, March, recently returned from her last overhaul at Darlington, on July 13th 1961. Photograph A.G. Ellis, www.transporttreasury.co.uk

60831 with **I & R Morley** excursion board (it was a Sutton in Ashfield firm) waiting to take back the happy campers, on Bridlington shed, 25th August 1956. Photograph A.G. Forsyth, Initial Photographics.

LNER 4803 when new was loaned to St. Margarets, and it is here that the V2 was photographed. After having been at most GN sheds, she became one of the New England hardy annuals, a regular sight on the main line. Photograph J. Robertson, www.transporttreasury.co.uk

60833 at Doncaster on 17th March 1963 (above) and below on York shed 2nd May 1964.

60833 shimmering fresh after overhaul, at Darlington shed, 23rd April 1961. Photograph H.D. Ramsey, Initial Photographics.

No.60833, once put up for naming, stored at York and unlikely to run again.

Two views of 60835 THE GREEN HOWARD, probably at York. The engine is well cleaned, while the period is before the dark green livery and the 'beer label' totem of 1957; 1952-56 would be a good bet.

THE GREEN HOWARD

ALEXANDRA PRINCESS OF WALES'S

Richmond station on April 3rd 1939, when 4806 (60835) was named **THE GREEN HOWARD**. This heartening level of public interest in such an event seems unimaginable today. Photograph www.transporttreasury.co.uk

The last V2 was 60836 of Dundee Tay Bridge, in the yard of the old Caledonian/LMS shed ('Dundee West', which had served as the diesel shed since about 1961) on August 29th 1965.

One of the most undignified sights at the very end of the transition from steam to diesel/electric traction was use of the last V2, 60836, on the two coach branch service from Alnmouth to Alnwick in 1965-66. 'Ludicrous' would not be putting it too strongly. A considerable rumbling noise could be heard on a still evening, no doubt from LNER officers including Gresley himself, spinning in their graves! Photograph S.C. Nash.

Just over a year old, Tay Bridge's first V2, 4807 (60836) assisted by a J38 0-6-0, is about to leave with an up express within a month of war, on August 6th 1939. She was one of the five fitted with a Melesco superheater regulator, as can be seen from the cover behind the chimney. The external rodding was on the driver's side, unlike the five post-war Peppercorn A2s. The use of a J38 with 4ft 8ins coupled wheels on express work was distinctly unusual, for obvious reasons, although 'express' was a relative term north of the Forth Bridge as far as Dundee.

York's 60837 heads a class H freight north of York on May 21st 1955. Photograph J. Robertson, www.transporttreasury.co.uk

Dundee's 60838 at Haymarket on October 15th 1955. It is some months since a general overhaul, but the V2 is superbly clean. Photograph J. Robertson, www.transporttreasury.co.uk

60841 at Hatfield on June 2nd 1962 with a Class C freight, passing a MetroCammel DMU on a suburban service.

Leicester's 60842 waits at Sheffield Victoria with the up South Yorkshireman probably in 1958, with another Gresley engine, class EM1 No.26049, in the adjacent platform. (A Gresley engine? Well, the prototype EM1 was built during Gresley's leadership, but I fear that he would not have approved of the bogie design with its traction motors at the extremity of the bogie!) Photograph www.transporttreasury.co.uk

By September 1958 60843 was at Tweedmouth. Here the V2 has worked a train of TPO vehicles, possibly the 10.30 from Waverley, into Newcastle Central, and is now making her way to Gateshead. The year would be about 1960. Photograph J. Robertson, www.transporttreasury.co.uk

No.60844 out of steam at York shed in the 1960s, almost certainly awaiting repairs. Photograph J.G. Walmsley, www.transporttreasury.co.uk

Above. Dundee's 60844 at Perth, her driver waiting for the Right Away. I would guess that her train is the 12.05 to Edinburgh, which ran as a class B stopping passenger, and from that platform the train would be going either to Edinburgh or Glasgow.

Left. New England's *bête noire*, 60845, heads a down fast freight off the down main on to the down goods at Crescent Junction, south of the station at Peterborough. Looking at the shadows, the train is almost certainly the 16.15 Dringhouses goods. Very interestingly, the date, April 23rd 1952, lies between the general overhaul at Doncaster in March-April of that year, and the testing at Swindon later. Quite how the V2 had managed with its fast freight from London would have been interesting to know, remembering the state it was in by the time it reached Wiltshire. Photograph R.H. Fullagar, www.transporttreasury.co.uk

The former West Riding V2, at the end of steam, in foreign land at Carlisle Kingmoor on Aug 9th 1965.Photograph Peter Groom.

The nameplate of 60847, not looking too bad for once, on 5th May 1963. Many V2s were in filthy condition for a lot of the time and the state of plates might be one reason why one or two chosen institutions turned down the offer of a plate for their 'own' engine – perhaps they knew only too well how it might end up. After all, it was intended as an honour and should have been kept as such. Some regiments, for instance, were most aggrieved in the 1960s at the state of 'their' plates. Note too, how the plates were not centred above the driving axle – a minor aesthetic blunder. Photograph www.transporttreasury.co.uk

Above. St.PETER'S SCHOOL, YORK standing in Grantham Shed yard on Aug 7th 1959 with an O2 and an A3 behind. *Below*. Now rebuilt with separate cylinders, St.PETER'S SCHOOL, YORK is at Top Shed on May 5th 1963. Photographs Peter Groom.

An up express leaves Edinburgh Waverley behind 60848 on August 29th 1953. The V2 was overhauled at Darlington a month earlier, which accounts for her excellent appearance, making a fine photograph. Photograph J. Robertson, www.transporttreasury.co.uk

Doncaster's 60852 on shed in May 1959; this was the locomotive that achieved one of the fastest V2 runs between Doncaster and Kings Cross.

60852 of Doncaster has probably been borrowed for a return trip to Grantham, and is setting off on August 27th 1958 for Kings Cross with what looks like a principal service. The V2 is just ex-works and in splendid condition. Photograph Peter Groom.

Doncaster's 60852 waiting at Grantham to take over a southbound express on August 27th 1958. Photograph Peter Groom.

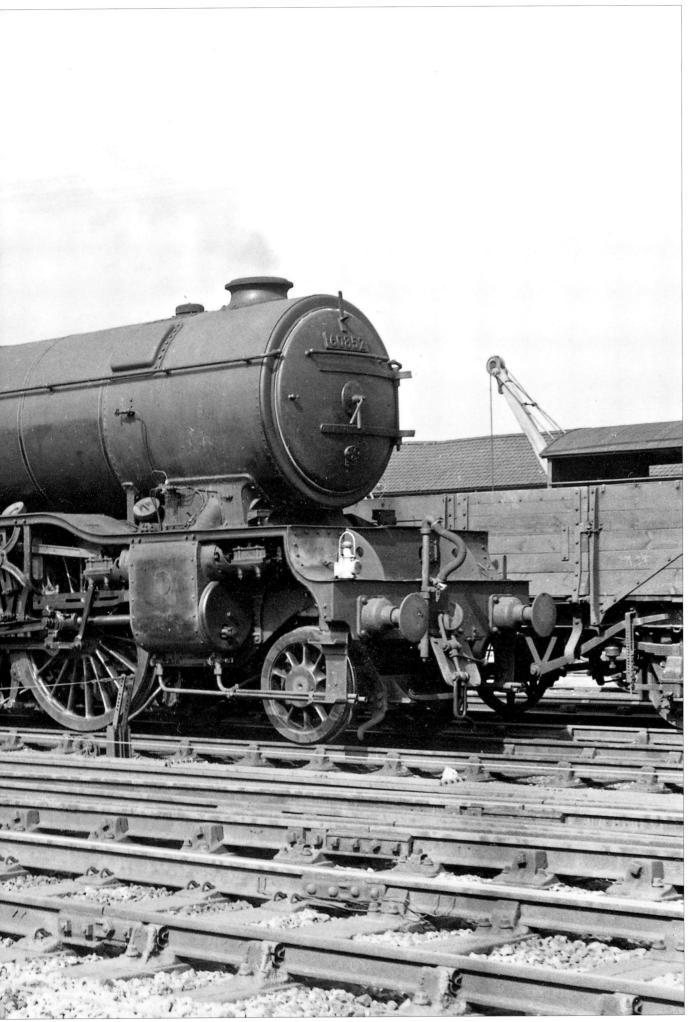

Yet another New England V2, 60853 with an up express on August 12th 1961. Clearly the effort of cleaning their locomotives in the last years of steam had proved too much for New England, at least in the case of this V2. The express looks to be one of the principal West Riding services.

Kings Cross V2 60854, without any hint of a copper-capped chimney, is fresh from general repair in 1959 at Darlington. Photograph www.transporttreasury.co.uk

Top Shed's 60854 heads a down express towards Hatfield at Red Hall on August 3rd 1962. Note the articulated twin behind the V2

No.60855, a one time Kings Cross engine had emigrated north to York in late 1958. Here she is in York Shed yard on May 16th 1964. Photograph Peter Groom.

60855 at York on 2nd May 1964.

Doncaster's 60857 waiting south of Grantham station to take over an up service on July 19th 1958. Photograph Peter Groom.

No.60857 at Doncaster shed on June 14th 1958. Photograph J. Robertson, www.transporttreasury.co.uk

It would be difficult for a locomotive to become blacker with dirt than New England's 60858. The Kylchap V2 is passing Wymondley, between Stevenage and Hitchin, on June 1st 1963. In the lower shot she has moved to Doncaster, where she is in the Shed yard on October 6th 1963.

60858, Doncaster, 6th October 1963.

60859 at Thornaby on 2nd May 1964.

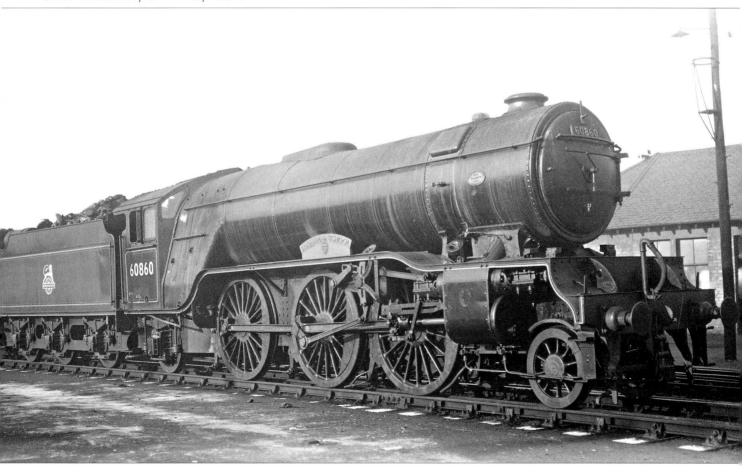

No.60860 DURHAM SCHOOL at Haymarket in early 1952, soon after overhaul at Darlington. Photograph W. Hermiston, www.transporttreasury.co.uk

A magnificent photograph of Top Shed's 60862, now fitted with a double Kylchap, heading the 16.15 York Dringhouses fast freight north of Wood Green Tunnel, on June 15th 1962. Photograph Peter Groom.

No.60862 was one of Top Shed's best V2s, over the years. Now as a Kylchap V2, she is at Kings Cross with another regular, No.60814, standing behind. Photograph Peter Groom.

No.60863 was a long-term GC section V2, and she is seen here at Banbury on May 5th 1953. Later the numberplate and smokebox handrail were transposed. Photograph www.transporttreasury.co.uk

60866, now rebuilt with separate cylinders, at Doncaster shed on July 1st 1962.

60866 at New England, March 31st 1963.

60867, now clearly a New England locomotive, with an up express passing Red Hall on August 12th 1961. This V2 was one of a small number of the class in which the smoke box numberplate and handrail were transposed.

New England's 60869 climbs to Stoke from the north.
I would plump for the 1952-55 period and the train
looks as if it might be the 14.55 from Hull, (No.579),
which grew shorter until it was amalgamated with the
15.40 from Hull, (No.581) using a Kings Cross B1.

No.60871 of New England, five months after general overhaul at Doncaster Works in good external condition – a rare phenomenon indeed. The date is August 19th 1962. She has been fitted with a lowered top headlamp bracket and numberplate, and the smokebox handrail has been replaced with two smaller ones. A number of V2s were modified in this way in the early 1960s in order to make access to the top lamp position safer. With V2s being withdrawn almost weekly, why did they bother? Photograph A.G. Forsyth, Initial Photographics.

No.60871 of Kings Cross with the 00.30 from Inverkeithing on the up goods between Connington South and Abbots Ripton in the later part of the 1950s. This was the balancing working of the 16.15 York goods the previous day.

60871 at Doncaster on 6th October 1963.

No.60872 KINGS OWN YORKSHIRE INFANTRY at Doncaster Shed. Apart from two months at Grantham in 1961, she was at Doncaster as her name required. The date is clearly after 1948 – numberplate and shedplate show that – but no later than the introduction of the later totem and green livery. There is little else to focus more exactly on the date. Although my own experience of KOYLI's running was best forgotten, she did not seem to be one of the regular runners as far as I remember. Photograph www.transporttreasury.co.uk

Apart from two months at Grantham in 1961, 60872 KINGS OWN YORKSHIRE LIGHT INFANTRY ('KOYLI') was a Doncaster engine, though it was not one of that shed's more prominent performers. Here she is on the wet ash pits at York shed on May 3rd 1962. Photograph Jack Hodgkinson.

60872 KINGS OWN YORKSHIRE LIGHT INFANTRY shimmering in black at Doncaster, six days after emerging from general overhaul, on August 9th 1956. As at every railway works/depot/shed, the workers lived close.

COLDSTREAMER, No.60873 at Haymarket shed on July 17th 1953. Photograph J. Robertson, www.transporttreasury.co.uk

COLDSTREAMER was one of the more elusive V2s. One might add 'even at Kings Cross'. In captioning hundreds of pictures, one can imagine a certain degree of correlation between numbers of illustrations and reliability of a particular machine. If it didn't get used so much, it would not have been available as a subject. 60873 seemed to be one such. However, John Robertson produced a beautiful study of this rather reclusive V2 leaving Moncrieff Tunnel at Hilton Junction with a miniscule Perth-Edinburgh fast freight. The engine alone would have outweighed its train and it is quite possible that the payload could have been carried by a single lorry, and not even an HGV at that! Photograph J. Robertson, www.transporttreasury.co.uk

No.60875, literally days from Doncaster Paint Shop, at Doncaster Station on an up service on August 1st 1953. I would imagine that she is running in, or ought to be. Although the headcode is "open lights" – express – what can be seen of the first vehicle suggests that it is a relief or excursion. The V2 looks superb. Photograph R.J. Buckley, Initial Photographics.

How are the mighty fallen! Doncaster's 60875 creeps into New England Yard with a slow freight in the period 1960-62. Photograph www.transporttreasury.co.uk

60875 braking for the curve south of Hatfield with a down express, August 12th 1961. By this time it had long since returned to Doncaster.

Top Shed had a relatively small group of Green Arrows, kept in good condition and well cleaned. This is an excellent illustration of a Kings Cross V2 in superb condition, passing through Doncaster with an up Class C fast freight, on August 4th 1955. The description on the original print refers to an up fish train, but those from Scotland passed Doncaster overnight, and those from Hull were hauled by K3s (or in the case of 581 up, a Top Shed B1 returning south) until replacement at Doncaster Decoy. It was more likely to be 273 up, the 00.30 from Inverkeithing, which was hauled from York to East Coast Goods Yard by a V2 with a 1A link crew. The footbridge was the main entrance to the Drawing Office and Works from the station. The central section had been renewed with a simple lattice structure spanning the platforms and four tracks. The old bridge had intermediate supports and the base of one is by the V2 tender. Photograph Eric Webb, www.transporttreasury.co.uk

No.60877 with one of the famous GC line 'Windcutters' on February 8th 1964 between Whetstone and Ashby Magna. In the background the old route of the Midland Rugby-Leicester line was being obliterated by earthworks for the new M1 motorway.

No.60880, fitted with a double Kylchap, with a down class H leaving New England yard. The train is unbraked and fairly lengthy. I would guess at 1963. Photograph B. Richardson, www.transporttreasury.co.uk

60880 with an up express in the cutting north of Sandy, July 25th 1959.

60880, its condition typical of the time and place, at New England on 24th March 1963.

A fine study of a Kylchap V2 with the modified front end, 60881 at New England in 1962. Photograph B. Richardson, www.transporttreasury.co.uk

Local V2 60881 crossing from the up main to the up platform road Doncaster station on August 9th 1956. Almost all activity at Doncaster took place south of the station, and I would imagine the V2 is about to take over the up service in the background.

60882 of St.Margarets on the climb out of Aberdeen to Cove Bay on April 18th 1958. The V2 easily outweighs her train of eight wagons and brake, which would hardly have embarrassed a J36 0-6-0, the smallest of the NBR 0-6-0s. The train would be meat for London and other cities, and I see that Aberdeen had run out of conflats. Photograph J. Robertson, www.transporttreasury.co.uk

No.60882 of St.Margarets, not long after her general overhaul, at St.Margarets on May 17th 1959. The shed was bisected by the main line to and from Waverley Station, a thoroughly dangerous arrangement. The two tracks in front of the V2 were the main line tracks. The up services in particular, descending the sharp gradient from Waverley, galloped round the curve through the depot at a good speed, and one needed to keep a sharp lookout if a premature end was to be avoided. Photograph R.J. Buckley, Initial Photographics.

No.60884 of Ardsley is at Saltersford, Grantham, on August 27th 1958. The train is almost certainly 264down, the 11.30 from Kings Cross Goods, which was used to return the empty "Blue Spot" long wheelbase fish vans back north. It looks as though the train has been stopped to judge from the V2's exhaust, as there was a colour light signal just to the left of the shot. Drainage work appears to be in hand at the time: the down side cutting slope gave trouble over the years and required remedial work. Photograph Peter Groom.

60885, a Thornaby engine, at Darlington on May 3rd 1962, fresh from the Works and a sight for sore eyes. Photograph Jack Hodgkinson.

The first V2 with modified front end, 60886 when at Heaton in May 1956.

60886 was a long-term Tyneside V2, but in 1962 she moved to York where she was photographed on 1st May 1966. She had been last overhauled three years earlier, with a light repair (that would not merit a repaint) six months earlier, so her cleanliness is unusual, to put it mildly.

Leicester V2 60890, stored under the shear legs there on May 20ᵗʰ 1962. She was actually withdrawn a few weeks earlier and the shear legs too must have lifted their last some time before. Photograph Jack Hodgkinson.

No.60893, a long-term New England engine, running light from York shed to the south end of the station. She was usually like this, but was one of those V2s that would appear on a busy Saturday, going a great deal faster than most other services. She had a short spell on the SR in 1953 along with five other V2s, but was well cleaned up beforehand!

The slightly unnerving sight of a clean New England V2, 60893 as we rarely saw her, well polished, with the down Bournemouth Belle approaching Basingstoke in May-June 1953. The loaned V2s had to have extra lamp irons to carry the more sophisticated SR route code description discs, and the front footsteps had to be removed and the cylinder drains secured specially to avoid fouling or draining on to the live rail.

New England's 60893 heads an up express past Red Hall on August 15th 1955. Still with the extra smokebox door lamp iron for the route description headcodes used on the SR.

60893, now with a separate middle cylinder, with a down express approaching Red Hall on August 12th 1961.

60897 within a few months of withdrawal at Doncaster Shed on March 17th 1963. MINORU is in the background.

March V2 60899 on shed on May 22nd 1955. Photograph J. Robertson, www.transporttreasury.co.uk

60899 with a down express north of Sandy, July 25th 1959.

York's 60901 getting a down fast freight moving past Hornsey on April 26th 1955. The first part of the Scots Goods, 262 down, was a York turn in several timetables, and I would say that it is this, or the 16.15 Dringhouses Goods an hour or so later, rather than the main train, 266 down.

60902 at Doncaster on 6th October 1963.

129

60902 was converted to double Kylchap, but by August 17th 1963 she was a Doncaster V2, seen here on York Shed. A month later she was withdrawn.

The 16.15 York goods accelerates north of Werrington Junction behind immaculate double Kylchap V2 60903 in 1962. At a time when express locomotives were becoming dirtier by the month, Kings Cross was the exception, with even the locomotives on freight lodging turns gleaming. Photograph B. Richardson, www.transporttreasury.co.uk

No. 60903, one of Top Shed's longest residents, gathers speed north of Finsbury Park with 714 down, the York Dringhouses fast freight, on May 30th 1960. This V2 had 14 months running, say about 60-70,000 miles, by the time this picture was taken, and ran just over another year before the next overhaul when the double Kylchap was fitted. Photograph Peter Groom.

60903, condemned and readied as a 2-4-2 for disposal, New England 31st March 1963.

60906 was one of New England's long time residents, seen here at York on May 25th 1952. Four months after general overhaul, she is in good condition. Photograph B.K.B. Green, Initial Photographics.

York's 60907, just out of shops, heads an up freight south of Northallerton. I would guess that this is just after the May 1961 overhaul. It is a very good study showing what a fine looking locomotive the V2 was in its original condition. Photograph www.transporttreasury.co.uk

The driver is oiling round 60912 of New England, with Top Shed's regular B1, 61139 and an A1 to the right. The year? I would guess about 1955. Photograph E.D. Bruton.

133

Copley Hill's 60913 heads a down express past Hornsey on April 16th 1952. The V2s at Leeds were there for the freight lodging turn, but at holiday times they were used on passenger duties.

The decline in standards as the elimination of steam drew nearer is obvious, as evidenced by 60914, once a well cleaned Top Shed regular, and now at New England. The up express is at Red Hall, south of Hatfield, on May 20th 1961. The first vehicle is an invader from the west, a 'Siphon H' I believe.

60914, once a smartly turned out Top Shed regular, but now condemned to a garb of 'BR grey' at New England, heading an up express at Red Hall, south of Hatfield, on August 12th 1961. The first vehicle is a corridor brake, reversed in the traditional GN main line fashion. The portions detached on the northward journey beyond Doncaster to the West Riding were returned later for attachment to up services, and obviously the coaches were not turned in the process; moreover they were not necessarily attached in a similar order, and gradually, one feels, the operating staff despaired of achieving the correct and orderly formation as with the North Country and Scottish services.

60915 has arrived at Woodford Halse from Top Shed two months before, and is seen here on March 4th 1951. The Darlington works plate has been joined by another BR plate on the front framing. Photograph B.K.B. Green, Initial Photographics.

A long-time resident of the GC, 60915 moved to Thornaby in September 1959. That depot had no main line passenger turns, but the rule on summer Saturday was 'if it'll go then we'll use it', and it has been borrowed, for a main line turn to Grantham in May 1961. The replacement A3 has moved out of the engine spur ready to reverse on to her train.

60918 at Sheffield Darnall shed, a seldom photographed place, on July 1ˢᵗ 1962. An infrequent sight down south, she had gone to York when new and stayed there until withdrawal in October 1962.

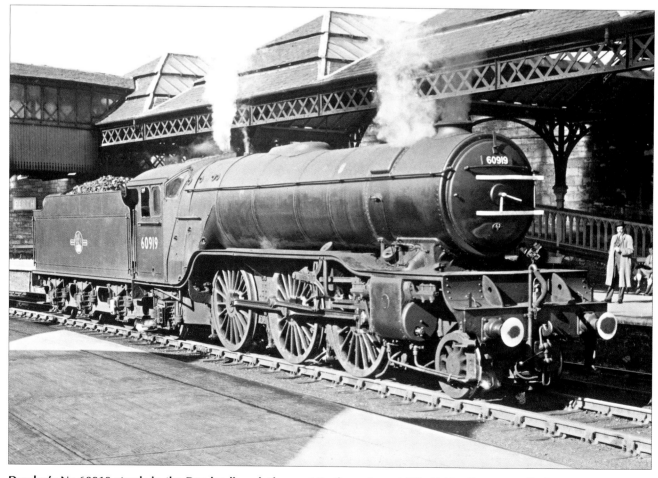

Dundee's No.60919 stands in the Dundee line platforms at Perth on August 15ᵗʰ 1966. She was well cleaned and the front decorated in order to work a number of railtours including one on the Southern Region, although in that case she ran hot on the long trek south and was stabled at Basingstoke pro tem. Photograph Paul Cotterell.

No.60919's driver has eased her regulator at Dalmeny for the speed restriction over the Forth Bridge. The date is unknown but would be in the mid-1950s. Photograph J. Davenport, www.transporttreasury.co.uk

Dundee's 60920, fresh from Darlington Works in 1948-49, makes a magnificent photograph. Photograph A.G. Forsyth, Initial Photographics.

Dundee's V2 60920 has been out of shops for nine months but has cleaned up remarkably well. Here she is at Dundee West on the turntable on October 12th 1955. Photograph A.W. Battson, www.transporttreasury.co.uk

In contrast to other, more uplifting pictures of 60920, here she is in store at Bathgate shed, on August 16th 1962. I doubt she ran again, and she was withdrawn in the night of the Accountants' Long Knives, December 29th 1962.

A Doncaster V2 but with the New England look, 60921 leans to the curve at Red Hall with a down express, almost certainly bound for Hull or Leeds, on August 12th 1961.

60921 at home at Doncaster on July 1st 1962; she was one of the batch that stayed in the south, and was at Carr Loco for much of the time.

Both photographs. 60924 a week or so after condemnation and awaiting entry to the nearby works for scrapping, Doncaster 6ᵗʰ October 1963.

60925 was always a York V2, and here on August 1st 1953 she has paused with an up stopping service at Selby. Photograph J. Robertson, www.transporttreasury.co.uk

Oh dear! The up Tees-Tyne Pullman rounds the south curve at Red hall, running about 50 minutes late behind No.60925. The up train had been hauled from Newcastle by 60028 WALTER K WHIGHAM which had run hot by York, where the pilot V2 came on as replacement. It was not a good day for the normally reliable A4, failing as it did for the fourth time in four weeks. It was not a good day for MALLARD either: her repairs at Gateshead needed more time and her place was taken on the up Flying Scotsman by 60019 BITTER.

60925 on shed at Darnall, July 1st 1962; like a number of her sisters, she went new to York and stayed there.

A pair of NE V2s, 60926 of Tweedmouth and 60923 of Gateshead stand outside Haymarket shed in 1961-62, with the new railway in the shape of an English Electric Type 4 alongside. Photograph W. Hermiston, www.transporttreasury.co.uk

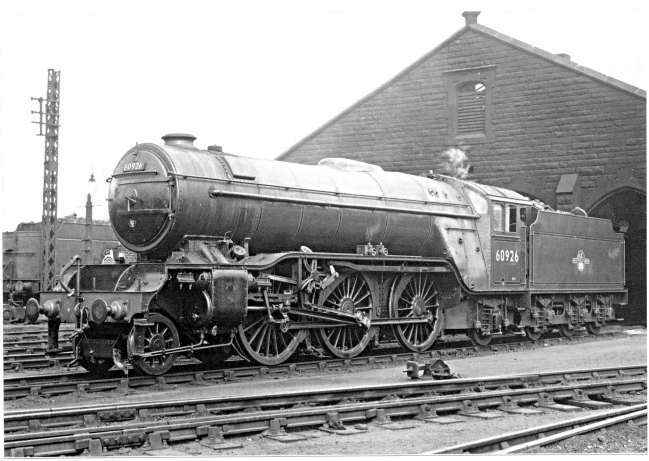

60926 was another Tweedmouth pilot engine, and is seen here on shed. No date is given, but I would plump for soon after the May 1957 overhaul. She is green but without any form of ATC. Photograph M. Robertson, www.transporttreasury.co.uk

On August 25th 1949 it is two years since 929 saw the inside of Darlington Works, and it certainly looks it. She is at York shed with another that looks as though she needs soling and heeling, with a new A1 alongside, probably 60129 or 60153 as it appears to be in BR blue livery. It was sometimes a problem to use a run-down locomotive to good purpose so as to work up the shopping mileage, but whatever their condition the V2s were rarely rough riders. Photograph F.W. Goudie, www.transporttreasury.co.uk

60929 moved to the NE Area from Doncaster, and stayed there. She is at York, on September 29th 1963. Photograph Jack Hodgkinson.

60929, Doncaster 17th March 1963.

146

60930 pilots Britannia 70035 THOMAS HARDY at York with a cross-country service in the late 1950s. Photograph www.transporttreasury.co.uk

60930 was always a Doncaster engine, and here she is no doubt running steadily, with a down ECS train just north of Biggleswade station on March 24th 1953. I would guess from the look of the elderly stock that it is the 11.15 Holloway-York ECS service, which was often used to send coaching stock north for repair or withdrawal.

No.60931 of **Tay Bridge** pounds up the 1 in 70 through North Queensferry with an up express on June 15th 1957. The fireman has some decent coal to use, but his predecessor didn't, to judge from the back of the coal space. It looks more suitable for a footpath. Photograph J. Robertson, www.transporttreasury.co.uk

No.60932 was always a NE Area V2, and spent over a dozen years in monastic seclusion at Tweedmouth as one of the pilots. It was a surprise to find, late in the steam era, that she had joined the large fleet at York, and it is from there that she reached Annesley shed in 1963. Photograph Canon Alec George, www.transporttreasury.co.uk

60932 at Doncaster on 17th March 1963.

A familiar location by Lincoln shed: York's 60934 ambles past with the cathedral in the background.

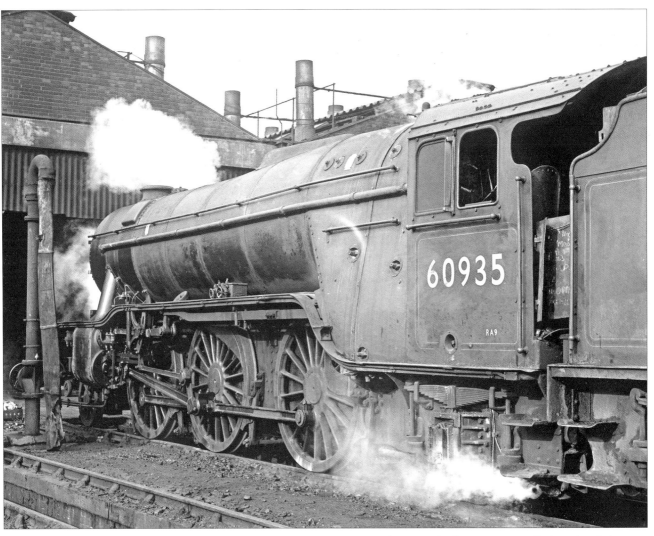

A long-term Doncaster engine, V2 60935 is on Carr Loco on February 24th 1963. She has separate cylinders, but it has not been thought necessary to fit a Smith speedometer. Photograph A.W. Battson, www.transporttreasury.co.uk

60936 comes under the brand new flyover bridge north of Sandy with an up express on July 25th 1959. The old bridge had been in need of repair for some while, and the debate over the future of the Bedford-Cambridge line was no nearer a conclusion. Eventually the Chief Civil Engineer must have declared 'thus far and no farther' and renewed it.

60936 was a long term New England engine, but she has by this time moved north to Doncaster; she is on a down express at the familiar location of Red Hall, near Hatfield, on August 12th 1961.

Dundee's 60937 is a magnificent sight, just fresh from Darlington Paint Shop on July 7th 1956. The shape of the covers to the main steam pipe changed over the years, certainly between Doncaster and Darlington, and 60937 appears to be without hers. Photograph A.R. Carpenter, www.transporttreasury.co.uk

Heaton's 60939 turns in one of the Neville Hill roundhouses (the far one is seen to have its roof removed) in 1957. B1 61069 and A3 TRIGO are in the background.

Gateshead V2 60940 in July 1955 with the empty stock of a down relief, passing Haymarket station. Photograph W. Hermiston, www.transporttreasury.co.uk

Apart from three months No.60941 was always a York engine. Some of York's fleet were more frequent visitors south, but No.60941 was more elusive. Here she is pulling away south of Grantham with a heavy train on September 19th 1955. Photograph Peter Groom.

The up Northumbrian gets under way behind Doncaster's No.60943 south of Grantham near Great Ponton on July 26th 1958. The use of a Doncaster engine was unusual. The up Northumbrian was the return working of the down Scots Goods, which points to a failure on either leg of the diagram. Photograph Peter Groom.

Top shed's 60943 races past that wonderful little signalbox, Greenwood, with an up express on August 10th 1957 shortly after my amazing run with her. She was well advanced in mileage by that time, but was clearly in fine condition. I would guess that she had been repaired at the shed and having been run in on light duties, was regularly turned out for summer passenger work. Photograph J. Robertson, www.transporttreasury.co.uk

60943 in the shed yard at Grantham by the shed 'stop' board (actually 'halt') near the yard exit in August 1958. She is coaled up ready for an up train (we are looking north here). Photograph Peter Groom.

My old friend of five years earlier, 60943 now at Doncaster, brings a light freight or parcels train south of Red Hall on August 3rd 1962. Like many of her sisters, the V2 now has the separate cylinder castings and wider outside main steam pipes.

Heaton's 60944 is on an up express, by the look of it a summer extra, formed of seven well matched LMS coaches. The train is near Grantshouse, and the time would probably be in the early 1950s. Photograph E.D. Bruton.

60944 in early 1949, not long after overhaul I would say, with the BR legend rather than the Ferret and Dartboard on the tender. The location is unclear and I shall need my Scottish friends to render assistance here. Craigentinny is suggested, but I do not recall many trees there. The distant chimney is like that at Haymarket; the V2 is standing in a yard of sorts, and a running line is in the distance to judge from the signal post. I pass. Photograph J. Robertson, www.transporttreasury.co.uk

No.60946 is being prepared for the road with the driver oiling round; bottles on the running plate by the firebox. The shed is York and the date May 23rd 1955. Photograph J. Robertson, www.transporttreasury.co.uk

Gateshead's 60947 sets out past King Edward Bridge Junction with semi-fast service on April 28th 1956. Photograph J. Robertson, www.transporttreasury.co.uk

After a long spell at March, 60948 has rejoined her sisters on the GN main line. Here, working from Grantham, coming directly out of the sun with a down express, she rounds Red Hall curve on August 3rd 1962. The V2 is filthy, made by the angle to look even worse.

60949 at St.Margarets shed, 17th August 1962. Always a Tyneside engine, it had joined a number of no-longer-wanted V2s at Tweedmouth by that summer.

60950 at Doncaster on 6th October 1963.

A GN main line V2 that was one of the Top Shed fleet for years. With impending dieselisation, 60950 has moved to Grantham – on June 1st 1963 she is approaching Grantham with a up class D fast freight. Photograph M. Castledine.

Above. 60950, now a Grantham engine, on shed there on August 15th 1962. Photograph Jack Hodgkinson.

Left. Haymarket was usually home for 60951, and her driver seems pleased at the choice of engine for his day. The clash between the livery design and the outer firebox washout plug is all too evident here. The detail of the Cortazzi axlebox is also clear, showing the inclined sliding surfaces. Photograph www.transporttreasury.co.uk

60952 inside Thornaby shed on 2nd May 1963.

LNER 3665 (60953) at an unknown location, though I'd plump for the outskirts of Edinburgh. I'd put the period at around 1942, a snatched shot prohibited under wartime regulations, which explains the less than perfect quality of the print. It is before the LNER legend was précised down to NE in which case, judging from her condition, 3665 was almost new.

No.953 at her home shed, Haymarket, between mid-1946 and mid-1948, in wartime black livery. Photograph www.transporttreasury.co.uk

The Aberdeen portion of a Kings Cross-Aberdeen service leaves The Mound Tunnel behind Ferryhill's 60955 on September 3rd 1959. The V2 is making a strong start for the last lap of a long journey. Photograph F.W. Goudie, www.transporttreasury.co.uk

St.Margarets' V2 60957 has just returned to Darlington for a minor tweak after a general overhaul, and is running in on an up freight past York shed on May 22nd 1959. She was for many years a NE engine and is on her old stamping grounds again. Photograph R. Wilson, www.transporttreasury.co.uk

A down parcels service passing Holloway South Down behind York's No.60961 in Autumnal weather on October 29th 1962. The train is probably the midday York parcels, 842 down. Photograph Peter Groom.

No less than thirteen of the last 24 V2s built were at York at the turn of the 1950s, a depot already with a sizeable V2 fleet. 60962 had moved north later, and is seen here at Heaton, her home shed, on May 3rd 1962. Photograph Jack Hodgkinson.

York's 60963 at Doncaster on July 1st 1962. It was one of the two V2s fitted with a double blastpipe, said to be similar to the Royal Scot design. The Doncaster double chimney sits well on a V2 with the original front end, and if anything has a more balanced appearance than on the A3s, where the presence of the superheater header forced the chimney too far forward, in my view.

York's No.60963 was one of the two V2s selected for experimental redraughting using a BR (Royal Scot) double blastpipe, in early 1960. Here she is "at home" in the yard at York on May 2nd 1963. I believe No.60963 was not the intended recipient of the double chimney, but I have not seen any corroborating evidence to support it.

60964 in the unlikely environs of Tyne Dock shed, 1 March 1963. Photograph Paul Cotterell.

The cabside plate of 60964, taken late in the life of the V2. The square ended plug low on the cabside of all large Gresley engines gave access to the rear corner of the firebox foundation ring, for washing out. The firebox was the hottest and most important part of the boiler heating surface and it was important to flush out the solids in the waterlegs and on the foundation ring. Photograph Paul Chancellor Collection.

No.60964 THE DURHAM LIGHT INFANTRY, in immaculate condition soon after its naming, at Haymarket on May 22nd 1958. Photograph M. Robertson, www.transporttreasury.co.uk

Gateshead's 60967 leaves Penmanshiel Tunnel running light in March 1955. The V2 would have to reach Tweedmouth before picking up a train. Photograph W. Hermiston, www.transporttreasury.co.uk

60968, another York fixture, swings past Red Hall with a down express on August 12th 1961.

Dundee's 60969 on foreign territory, at St.Rollox, otherwise known as Balornock, the former LMS shed on the north side of Glasgow, on June 16th 1957. She would have worked from Dundee, possibly from Dundee West, via Perth, or perhaps Ferryhill borrowed a V2 in good condition for one of the Aberdeen-Glasgow expresses. Again, good coal at the front and not at the back. I have often wondered who St.Rollox was. Not the patron saint of three cylinder locomotives, certainly. Photograph J. Robertson, www.transporttreasury.co.uk

60970, one of the late withdrawals in the class, at St.Margarets on April 9th 1962. For much of her time she was an Aberdeen engine, but broke new ground in June 1960 as one transferred to Perth. Later at St.Margarets she was a familiar sight on the Waverley route amongst others.

Dundee Tay Bridge's No.60971 at Haymarket on August 13th 1955, just after a recent visit to Darlington Works. BR introduced a small works plate which seemed to be used to replace the brass if it had been – er – mislaid. Whether BR, in a moment of corporate stupidity, had sought to eradicate traces of previous ownership, as in the case of MALLARD's plaque in 1948, one cannot tell.

The 17.36 pulls away from Dundee behind 60972 of Tay Bridge on May 7th 1955. Photograph J. Robertson, www.transporttreasury.co.uk

Dundee's 60972 in happier days, August 3rd 1952, at Dundee Tay Bridge. A Class J88 shunter with wooden block buffers is to the left, and a D49 Shire 4-4-0 to the right, 62708 ARGYLLSHIRE.

In its decline, NE Region V2s were a far more common sight on the GC section than in earlier days. Here York's 60975 leaves Rugby Central with the 17.15 Nottingham Victoria-Marylebone on July 3rd 1963. Photograph Jack Hodgkinson.

No.60978 has been borrowed from York by Neville Hill to work the up Queen of Scots Pullman, and John Robertson's splendid photograph, on May 18th 1954, shows a well cleaned V2 at Gateshead (ironically) before taking over. Photograph J. Robertson, www.transporttreasury.co.uk

York's V2 has been transferred to Darlington and is on shed on August 4th 1953, presumably as pilot, by the look of the well-filled tender. Photograph J. Robertson, www.transporttreasury.co.uk

60982 at Doncaster on 6th October 1963.

A superb study by John Robertson at Kings Cross shed, April 30th 1958. Top Shed had the first and the last V2s, and 60983 was one of their hard-working regulars on passenger turns. Doncaster repaired ER V2s until 1957, and methods of repairing the small main steam pipe between the saddle and piston valve and its cover differed between works. Photograph J. Robertson, www.transporttreasury.co.uk

With one month to go before withdrawal, 60813 stands by the coaling stage at St.Margarets on August 23rd 1966. She seems to have been a well-regarded locomotive and Dundee have kept her in good condition. Photograph Peter Ward.

CHAPTER TEN
EPILOGUE

The group of notes reproduced in Appendix E probably illustrates the role of the Green Arrows post-war on the East Coast Route as well as any written description. It shows that the main line would have been very difficult to operate without them. Not impossible, but crews would have been forced to become much more familiar with the rigours of the B1s than they would have liked. The ex-LNER Regions had a surplus of large locomotives, and it was impossible to utilise them all fully. The Thompson Pacifics were probably the worst example of under-utilisation, but there were insufficient diagrams making full use of the V2s as well. Of course it would have had important implications in terms of artisan staffing and materials at depots to keep the timetable running with fewer locomotives, together with investment in such as roller bearings and manganese liners to reduce wear and overheating. This allowed the operation of the main line without resort to the B1 4-6-0s except where RA9 locomotives were barred.

There is no doubt that the V2s in their time moved a mountain of freight traffic as well as any other locomotive class and probably better than any other. But with the shadow of dieselisation looming, it was decided that the V2s could be replaced by the Class 9F 2-10-0s,

themselves also a remarkably good design, newer and simpler. In February 1962 New England's 60850, one of their best, was withdrawn. By New Year 1963 there had been a wholesale withdrawal of 69 locomotives, more than a third of the class. The last V2, 60836, was withdrawn on the last day of 1966, after the indignity of working the Alnwick two-coach branch train!

As previously discussed, they were slightly too large for the needs of the LNER at that time, and an RA7 design with say 75-80% of the V2's potential would have been more appropriate. In an ideal world post-war, with a smaller boiler and double Kylchap, they could have been used on lighter classified routes such as the GE lines. And yet within three years history made nonsense of that view, for the presence of numbers of large engines in wartime was a life saver for the LNER. Gresley's engines did not fare too well in wartime conditions, but the V2s did better than most. They were new, and their size meant that they could cope with heavy tasks without breaking down. The overall speed limit of 60 mph and slower schedules in wartime reduced the incidence of overheating at a time when under-maintenance would have tended to increase failures. The V2, perhaps with less pressure from working the principal

fast and heavy services, accumulating mileage at a lower rate, was less prone to overheating than the other large Gresley engines. Economical and easy riding, the crews were fond of them, and a turn on a Green Arrow, so long as it had not been hobbled with self-cleaning apparatus, was an easy day.

Fortunately, even the BRB recognised the importance and worth of the V2, and that is why GREEN ARROW herself is preserved. She is a memory to us who knew the steam era, and an example to those who did not, of just what a fine looking locomotive Gresley produced. Some years ago she visited the Bodmin and Wenford preserved railway, and it was a culture shock to see her among the panniers and industrial tanks at Bodmin. Clearly the local crews had difficulty with the Gresley regulator in many cases, but one man at least had the right idea with a generously open regulator and short cut-off, and Cornwall resounded to the familiar sound of a V2 working hard. 'Better than a King' was not a remark that I expected. Her valves had been set at Norwich by the master, the late Bill Harvey, and she sounded as perfect a V2 as I have heard. But not like the V2 of our memories with their distinctive eccentric exhaust beat, a sound we shall long remember.

60946 at Thornaby on 2nd May 1963.

Not what she was designed for. BANTAM COCK heads for Glasgow past Saughton Junction on June 1st 1951 with a short freight. The fireman has just completed a round of firing by the look of the exhaust. Photograph John Robertson, www.transporttreasury.co.uk

BANTAM COCK on April 5th 1952; the location is noted as 'Bedford Road Sidings' but it is unknown to me and I suspect it is somewhere close to Eastfield shed where the V4 was allocated. Photograph John Robertson, www.transporttreasury.co.uk

CHAPTER ELEVEN
THE BANTAMS - THE V4

After the first batch of five V2s had entered service, there was no doubt a period of assessment. By 1939 work had started at Doncaster on a small Prairie design. One might speculate that the operators had requested a locomotive with much wider route availability. For all its qualities, the V2 was not an answer to the coming crisis for the LNER operators, which as much as the war was due to the life-expiry of designs that had still been serviceable at Grouping. With the formation of the LNER in 1923, Gresley had inherited a number of good designs from the pre-Grouping companies. He continued to use these and in fact enlarged some classes but by the 1940s, a locomotive half-life later, mid-life had become old age.

A new design was needed to work services off the main line to routes where the V2 was too large and from which it was prohibited. The first design was one in which weight was a prime consideration. A new tapered boiler was mated with 5ft 2in coupled wheels, and very untypically for a Gresley design, it had two cylinders. It was superseded by a second design in which the wheel diameter was increased to 5ft 8in and a third cylinder added. The tapered boiler was intended to work at 300psi, which enabled the reduction of the cylinder size.

The third design, which was built, was similar but the working pressure was reduced to 250psi. The Diagram 112 boiler was formed of nickel steel plate, fitted with the normal Doncaster round-top firebox and a wide grate. The three cylinders were 15x26in, and their 7in piston valves were driven by Gresley's conjugated gear. Two locomotives were built, and the opportunity was taken with the second to use a steel firebox with a Nicholson thermic siphon. This was a device used in Europe and the USA to improve water circulation, which also enabled the evaporation rate to recover more quickly after a stop or check. The steel inner firebox and thermic siphon was removed after four years running when repairs were needed. The pair were coupled to Group Standard 5½ ton, 3500 gallon tenders, similar to those coupled to the K4 2-6-0s. The locomotive weight had to be kept as low as possible, and apart from the use of alloys in construction, the tender water tanks were of welded construction as was that of COCK O THE NORTH in 1934.

Due to the onset of war, construction at Doncaster was not completed until early 1941. As the engines were intended for mixed traffic their construction was not stopped but materials were in short supply with the outbreak of war, especially the alloys, sophisticated for

those times. Both V4s were outshopped in LNER apple green livery, since the wartime black livery did not come into force until November of that year. The first engine, No.3401, was named BANTAM COCK, and was inspected at York instead of Marylebone, together with the prototype EM1 Bo-Bo 1500v DC locomotive, No.6701 (later BR 26000).

BANTAM COCK was allocated first to Doncaster in March and tested over the difficult line to Leeds, which was RA9 and therefore open to the largest designs. It was then moved to York in April where a number of lighter routes were available, but within three weeks it was moved to Haymarket where it worked to Perth. After some heating problems, she was loaned for a fortnight to Kittybrewster in June, working the Deeside branch to Ballater and the coastal route north to Peterhead and Elgin, all routes which were RA4 if not RA3 in the case of the Deeside branch.

By June No.3401 had moved to the GE Section at Stratford, working passenger and freight to Ipswich, Southend, Cambridge and Whitemoor. She remained at Stratford until November 1941, when she moved to Norwich. The work of BANTAM COCK on the GE was surprisingly good for a small locomotive. Wartime loads had increased to the 450-500 ton level, far

A weary BANTAM COCK backing on to Eastfield shed at some time between 1946 and 1949 when she was painted in BR lined black. In contrast, it might be said, to the immaculate apple green 'Director' in the background. Photograph www.transporttreasury.co.uk

bigger than the GE had experienced before, and the ability of a locomotive that on first sight looked rather less powerful than a B17 or B12, was impressive. Indeed the ability of the V4 to handle main line passenger loads and keep time on admittedly slow wartime schedules was a feature of experience elsewhere at the other depots.

During that time the second V4 had been completed, unofficially known as 'BANTAM HEN' and allocated to Doncaster where a number of secondary routes were available for testing. Nothing is known of her running at Carr Loco. In September 1941 she moved to Eastfield where she took up working on the West Highland Line. Meanwhile in February 1942 BANTAM COCK moved back to Haymarket again, and in October 1943 to Eastfield to join her sister.

Their work on the West Highland brought them alongside the three cylinder, 5ft 2in K4 2-6-0s, the ex-GNR two cylinder 'Ragtimer' K2 2-6-0s and the NBR 'Glen' 4-4-0s. The K4s had a considerably greater tractive effort, and were better on the heavy gradients and curves with a heavy freight. The K2s could stand no end of pounding and would be ready for more, but their load hauling capacity was less than the three cylinder engines, and normally they worked as pilots or in tandem. On the easier roads south of Craigendoran, the K2s could gallop if their crews could hang on, but the K4s were limited to 45mph, and in their normal state sounded as if that was 15mph too fast.

The V4s offered a vastly better ride, a comfortable cab, and if handled properly, plenty of power. On a route that could hardly be more difficult, through country that was not green without good reason, where snow and frost were commonplace, these were very important considerations. To the Fort William men that I have met over the years it was as good a steam locomotive as they ever had on the line, and comparable to a Black Five or B1 4-6-0. One or two older drivers felt that they were the best that they had handled on the line. The first batch of Stanier Black Fives on the West Highland were poor, but they were sent away and their replacements were good. Like the Eastfield B1s which also came to work the line, despite the harder ride the 4-6-0s were larger and more sure-footed.

All West Highland ex-LNER engines were overhauled at Cowlairs, which before and during the 1939-45 war had a deservedly awful reputation, and although corrective action was taken, bad habits take root quicker than good ones and many of the Scottish ex-LNER locomotives made noises one suspected that they should not. A penalty for the V4s was a lengthy downtime for overhaul, and with the Black Fives, B1s and K1s now in command of the West Highland, both V4s were sent to Ferryhill in May 1954. They were used mainly on freight, but within three months had again been displaced by Black Fives, and so were loaned on to Kittybrewster in September 1954. Their work here took them around the GNofS routes, their weight only precluding them from two lines. A year later they returned to Ferryhill, and resumed the freight work to Dundee, Edinburgh and Perth, with the occasional passenger turn.

No spare boilers were made, unsurprisingly in wartime, but the flanging blocks for constructing replacements had unfortunately been scrapped. In March 1957 I suspect that the work on boiler 29558 was uneconomic, and since there were no spare boilers it was decided to scrap BANTAM COCK, and in November of the same year BANTAM HEN followed.

Below. 'BANTAM HEN' leaving Perth with a stopping service on September 3rd 1955. The Ferryhill V4 is heading south, possibly to Edinburgh, Glasgow or through Fife, all of which might seem odd for an Aberdeen locomotive. Photograph www.transporttreasury.co.uk

Top right. Eastfield's 61701 in foreign territory across the Clyde at Polmadie on August 3rd 1952. The V4 is dwarfed by BR Class 6 Pacific CLAN STEWART alongside, an interesting contrast aesthetically. Photograph B.K.B. Green, Initial Photographics.

Bottom right. 61701 in dishevelled condition at Eastfield. The date is between 1948 and 1954.

BANTAM COCK under construction in late 1940 in Doncaster Works. I am not familiar with the V4 design, but from the photograph the outside cylinders appear to be separate and not part of a monobloc casting, although it is difficult to be sure. Complex steel castings would surely have been impossible to obtain in wartime conditions.

BANTAM COCK, now an Eastfield engine, on the turntable there a month or so from a general overhaul at Cowlairs in March 1949. The V4s had a dome with a 'banjo' tail for steam collection. She was a handsome and, for her size, powerful machine. Photograph John Robertson, www.transporttreasury.co.uk

CHAPTER TWELVE
REFLECTIONS - THE V4

It is a sad little story, especially for a Gresley romantic. There is no doubt that the V4 was a promising design. But how on earth Gresley could have continued the development of what was a sophisticated design not only with war imminent, but on into the darkest hours of that war, with a rapidly changing and dangerous situation, shows how far he was losing touch, sadly.

It may sound strange from an engineering viewpoint but the V4 was a truly beautiful design. When engineers have lost sight of the importance of appearance and aesthetics alongside functionality, they have lost their way. It was, in miniature, a summary of all the features that made Gresley's locomotives

so pleasing aesthetically; the elegance, the balance, the *look* of locomotives designed for speed. It was a locomotive that any engineer would have been proud to put his name to.

Like all designs I think it would have needed 'tweaking' to achieve its best. Of the small amount of anecdotal evidence of the V4s' running, there were doubts only as to the ability of an inexperienced fireman to cope. And as they were intended for secondary routes, it was likely to happen more often than on the main line. I think that was probably due to a less than fully effective exhaust, which would hardly be surprising since with the quality of coal post-war the single blast Pacifics and V2s were handicapped until

redraughting. Not that I am advocating a double chimney, but a single Kylchap of either the 1K/T or 1K/1C design, probably within the existing chimney casting, would have provided a much stronger draught and not affect the appearance. The front pony truck was controlled by swing links, and with the certainty of travelling over lighter and less well maintained tracks substitution of the later V2 pattern truck would have been a wise precaution. Not that all secondary routes were poorly maintained – the quality of country staff was usually excellent and some country routes were very well kept.

Whether it was what the LNER needed in 1941 is a different matter altogether. It was not what Edward Thompson wanted, and he cancelled the order for another ten. Any parts made in anticipation would have quickly been consumed in the war effort. His B1 4-6-0 was a more effective answer, but it was an RA5 locomotive and not RA4 as was the V4. Even then there were a number of features adopted with the B1 to save weight, and the engines gave a hard ride as a result, that got harder and rougher as the mileage increased. The last 40 were built with manganese liners, and were more reliable and rode better as a result. One might wonder why the remainder were not so dealt with. One summer at Kings Cross, a top link crew had to work the 18.40 to Grimsby Town with its B1 as far as Peterborough while the other top link crew went to Newcastle with 'their' A4. The Lords of Creation, as Gerry Fiennes jokingly called the top link drivers, were not impressed. Some of the comments about old Bongos do not bear publishing. George Graham, of SILVER FOX, had his B1 going nicely below Hitchin at 85mph, when the violence of the bouncing blew the floorboards right out and the fireman was left standing on the framework contemplating the GN main line flying beneath his feet!

The railways were run on the basis of paying poor wages, providing little training at depot level, often minimal staff facilities and investing little in modern equipment. Although the financial management of the day might have been better, the LNER in particular was far from wealthy. Engineers worked hard to maintain machines of increasing sophistication in circumstances that were often Victorian, and it is remarkable that more did not give up the fight. The situation cried out for more modern depots and more equipment to avoid unpleasant and dangerous jobs. There were certainly areas off the main line where three cylinders were one too many, and there were even depots where

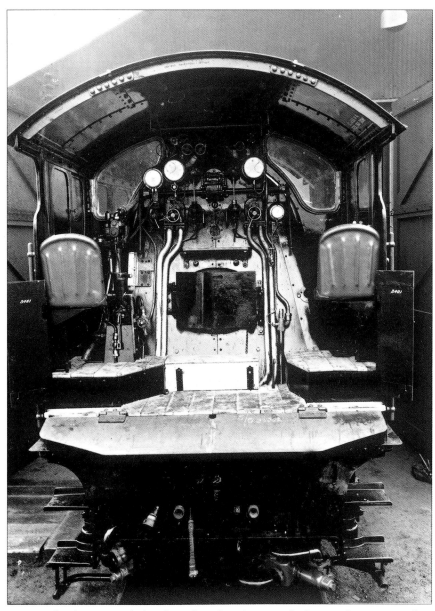

Construction has proceeded to the point where in 1941, the locomotive was complete and painted. Here one can see the good standard of accommodation the crew of the V4 had, certainly likely to appeal to the footplate staff at Fort William.

'BANTAM HEN', LNER No.1701, at Eastfield between June 1946, when her tender was exchanged with her twin, and June 1948 when she was repainted in apple green livery. Photograph John Robertson, www.transporttreasury.co.uk

one seemed more than enough! So often between inspections, the system relied on the driver reporting something amiss and if he didn't, or the fitting staff failed to deal with the problem in time, then there was another expensive failure on the road. The brutal truth is that a class of V4s would have been at work in the railway world off the main line in that sort of unforgiving environment. At Top Shed, Grantham, Norwich and Haymarket, for example, they would have prospered. Elsewhere, in the world of clattering motion, unlined grime and burnt smokebox doors, they certainly would not.

However, despite the cold douche of realism, it is a pity that the ten on order were not built, for there were places where a V4 would have been appreciated and put to useful work. In East Anglia and Lincolnshire they would have been useful replacements for obsolete locomotives and on the faster trains, a far more comfortable proposition than a wild-riding K3. Even the M&GN? The Hull and New Clee fast fish services would have been ideal for a V4.

I think that had the 2-6-2 been built as a two cylinder machine, the design might have prospered. It would have been excellent for the operation of the lighter engineered branches, enabling the elimination of numbers of elderly designs, and without imposing an extra burden on maintenance staff. A more intriguing thought is that if the V4, entirely theoretically of course, were

adapted to meet Edward Thompsons's principles, it would have been a half-size Pacific with divided drive and separate valve gears, a bogie in place of the pony truck – not as an elongated front end of course. It could have been a potent middle range locomotive and arguably better riding. So much for hindsight, however.

There is no doubt that there was skill and insight in the design, and now in the world of preserved steam, a BANTAM COCK would be worth its weight in gold. It would be light, strong enough, fast enough to go out on the main line, and although there is no hard evidence, almost certainly an economical locomotive. The K4 was soon ousted under BR and withdrawn in ignominy, but preservation of THE GREAT MARQUESS has shown us how excellent Gresley's smaller designs were, given the correct skilled attention.

When the A1 team at present engaged in replicating Arthur Peppercorn's A1 has completed its task with TORNADO, it should not be stood down or allowed to drift away in the best of BR traditions, but set to work on a new V4 project without delay.

Right. **'The Hen' in LNER apple green at Eastfield, evidently at work on the West Highland, to judge from the buffer beam snowplough. She had the LNER livery from June 1948 to September 1949. Photograph John Robertson, www.transporttreasury.co.uk**

No.61701 pulls out of Aberdeen Yard with the 06.25 goods to Laurencekirk on June 20th 1957. The V4s had been ejected from the West Highland by the summer of 1956 and, although useful locomotives still with more than half their life ahead, both engines had only a year or so left. The world of motive power had to be hard and unsentimental, for although many engineers in it took an enthusiastic pride and interest in their work, there was a service to run punctually, reliably and safely. Running two fairly unique locomotives was a chancy business. Inspections, repairs and the supply of spares always told against singletons with increased downtime and it was hardly surprising – if regrettable – that with diesels not far off, they were condemned. Photograph R. Wilson, www.transporttreasury.co.uk

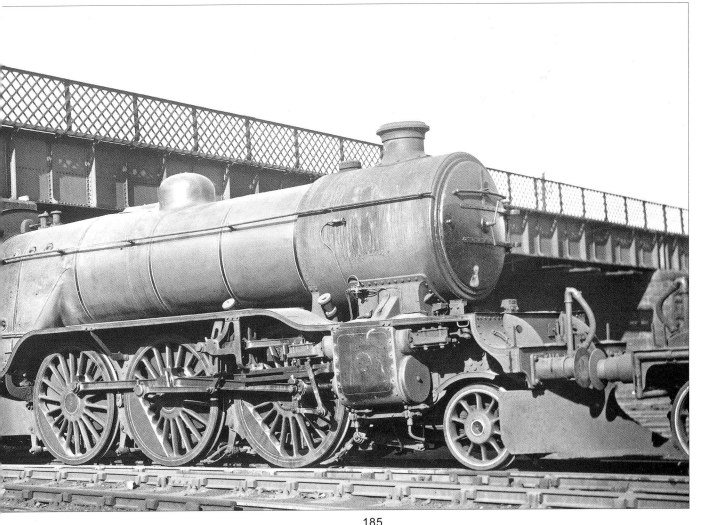

APPENDICES

APPENDIX A: V2 and V4 DIMENSIONS		
	V2	V4
Introduced	1936	1941
Boiler:-		
Boiler Diagram no.	109.00	112 (3401), 113 (3402)
Boiler Pressure	220	250
Grate Area	41.25	28.50
Max Outside Diameter	6ft5ins	5ft 4ins
Min Outside Diameter	5ft9ins	4ft 8ins
Tube length	16ft 11.625in	13ft 6ins
No. tubes	121	143
No. superheater flues	43	22
Boiler Heating Surface Area:-		
Firebox	215.00	151.60
Thermic Siphon		19.5 (3402 only)
Tubes	1211.57	884.30
Flues	1004.50	408.20
Subtotal (Evaporative)	2431.07	1444.1/ 1463.6
Superheater	679.67	355.80
Total	3110.74	1799.9(3401)/ 1819.4(3402)
Wheel Diameter:-		
Bogie	3ft 2ins	3ft 2ins
Coupled	6ft 2ins	5ft 8ins
Trailing	3ft 8ins	3ft 2ins
Cylinders (3)	18.5 x 26	15 x 26
Valves:-		
Piston Valve Diameter (all variations)	9ins	7ins
Travel (ins)	5.63	6.06
Lap (ins), Steam/Exhaust	1.625/0	
Lead (ins)	0.13	
Clearance volume as % swept volume	7.7% approx	
Tractive Effort (85% boiler pressure)	33730.00	27420
Single Blastpipe orifice (ins)1936	5.5/ 23.76sq.ins	17.72
1952	5.625/ 24.85sq.ins	
1953	5.375/22.69sq.ins	
Double Blastpipe orifice (ins) LMR 196	2x4.0/ 25.14sq.ins	
Kylchap 1960	2x5.25/ 39.27sq.ins	
Tender details		
Type	Group standard	
Coal (tons)	7.10	6.00
Water (gallons, nominal)	4200 (3,800 actual)	3500
Weight (tons)	52	42.75
Maximum axle load	22	17
Adhesive weight (tons)	65.60	48.55
Adhesive factor	4.36	3.97
Engine weight (tons)	93.10	70.40
Coupled wheelbase		12.83
Wheelbase length	56.18	29.33
Total length	66.43	59ft 9ins
Total locomotive weight	145.10	113.15

APPENDIX B LOCOMOTIVE DETAILS

BR No.	1946 LNER No.	Original LNER No.	Built	With-drawn	Notes	Works No.
60800	800	4771	13/6/36	21/8/62	NM	DR1837
60801	701/801	4772	8/8/36	1/10/62	SC9/52	DR1841
60802	802	4773	3/10/36	5/3/64	MC5/57	DR1843
60803	803	4774	30/10/36	16/6/63	MC8/61	DR1845
60804	804	4775	28/11/36	5/12/63		DR1846
60805	805	4776	16/7/37	23/12/63		
60806	806	4777	6/8/37	4/9/66	MC10/57	
60807	807	4778	24/8/37	19/11/62		
60808	808	4779	9/9/37	5/10/64	MC2/57	
60809	709/809	4780	31/8/37	6/7/64	NM11/9/37, MC1/62	
60810	710/810	4781	3/9/37	21/11/65	SC8/52, SC7/54	
60811	711/811	4782	10/9/37	23/4/62		
60812	812	4783	18/9/37	9/7/64	SC8/52	
60813	813	4784	27/9/37	29/6/66	DF12/46	
60814	714/814	4785	8/10/37	19/4/63	MC9/61	
60815	815	4786	20/10/37	30/4/62		
60816	816	4787	26/10/37	22/10/65	MC6/61	
60817	817	4788	1/11/37	16/6/63	DB3/60	
60818	718/818	4789	8/11/37	22/8/66		
60819	719/819	4790	15/11/37	29/12/62		
60820	720/820	4791	23/11/37	20/6/62	SC1/54	
60821	721/821	4792	3/12/37	29/12/62	MC2/58	
60822	722/822	4793	9/12/37	7/12/64	MC9/58	
60823	823	4794	21/12/37	26/3/62		
60824	824	4795	22/12/37	26/9/66	MC2/61	
60825	825	4796	6/1/38	27/4/64	MC7/60	
60826	826	4797	12/1/38	12/4/62		
60827	827	4798	18/1/38	29/12/62		
60828	828	4799	28/3/38	4/10/65	MC10/58	
60829	729/829	4800	1/4/38	31/5/62		
60830	830	4801	13/4/38	16/6.63	SC11/46, MC11/58	
60831	831	4802	30/5/38	6/12/66	MC6/57	
60832	832	4803	22/7/38	29/12/62	SC11/46	
60833	733/833	4804	31/8/38	25/5/64	ST, NMX, MS, MC4/61	
60834	834	4805	9/9/38	19/3/64	ST, MS	
60835	835	4806	23/9/38	19/10/65	ST, NM24/9/38, MS, MC3/62	
60836	836	4807	23/9/38	31/12/66	ST, MS,MC6/59	
60837	837	4808	5/10/38	16/11/65	ST, MS, MC 4/59	
60838	838	4809	11/10/38	23/1/64	ST, MC2/60	
60839	839	4810	19/10/38	22/10/62	ST,	
60840	840	4811	28/10/38	29/12/62	ST,	
60841	841	4812	18/11/38	22/9/63	ST, SC8/51, MC8/59	
60842	842	4813	9/12/38	22/9/63	ST,	
60843	843	4814	30/12/38	4/10/65	ST, MC5/58	
60844	844	4815	3/2/39	8/11/65		
60845	845	4816	22/2/39	23/9/62	SW, SC8/52, MC7/59	
60846	846	4817	17/2/39	19/10/65	MC6/57	
60847	847	4818	6/3/39	29/6/65	NM3/4/39, SC12/53, MC11/61	
60848	848	4819	3/3/39	16/7/62		
60849	849	4820	10/3/39	12/4/62	SC12/52	
60850	750/850	4821	17/3/39	26/2/62	SA12/60	
60851	851	4822	24/3/39	29/12/62		
60852	852	4823	31/3/39	22/9/63	SC1/54, SA11/60, MC10/61	
60853	853	4824	11/4/39	22/9/63	SA 1/60	
60854	854	4825	19/4/39	16/6/63	CC10-12/52, SC12/52, SA 11/60,	
60855	855	4826	21/4/39	13/4/64	MC1/59	
60856	856	4827	2/5/39	25/5/64	MC8/58	
60857	857	4828	10/5/39	17/4/62		
60858	858	4829	16/5/39	6/10/63	SC7/51, SC2/54, DBK10/61	
60859	859	4830	18/5/39	20/9/65	MC10/59	
60860	860	4831	26/5/39	22/10/62	NM15/6/39	
60861	861	4832	6/6/39	12/8/63	MC3/59	
60862	762/862	4833	13/6/39	16/6/63	MC3/57, DBK10/61	
60863	863	4834	19/6/39	23/4/62		
60864	864	4835	26/6/39	16/3/64		
60865	865	4836	29/6/39	14/6/65	MC11/59	
60866	866	4837	6/7/39	29/12/62	SC5/52, MC10/60	
60867	867	4838	20/7/39	1/5/62		
60868	868	4839	31/7/39	26/9/66	MC10/58	
60869	869	4840	10/8/39	16/6/63	SC5/52, MC7/61	
60870	870	4841	12/8/39	16/7/63	SC4/52	
60871	771/871	4842	1/9/39	22/9/63		
60872	872	4843	22/4/39	22/9/63	NM20/5/39, SA9/60	DR1898
60873	873	4844	18/5/39	29/12/62	NM20/6/39	DR1899
60874	874	4845	27/6/39	22/8/62		DR1900
60875	875	4846	28/7/39	5/3/62		DR1901
60876	876	4847	30/5/40	19/10/65	MC4/59	DR1912
60877	877	4848	26/6/40	13/2/66	SC2/54, MC1/59	DR1913
60878	878	4849	12/7/40	22/10/62	SC8/51, SC10/53	DR1915
60879	879	4850	6/8/40	3/12/62		DR1916
60880	880	4851	4/9/40	22/9/63	SC3/54, DBK8/61	DR1917
60881	881	4852	12/10/40	16/6/63	MC9/58, DBK 10/60	
60882	882	4853	7/10/39	13/7/64		
60883	883	4854	20/10/39	25/2/63	SC3/54	
60884	884	4855	27/10/39	6/9/65	SC5/54, MC9/56	
60885	885	4856	10/11/39	6/9/65		
60886	886	4857	18/11/39	10/4/66	MC5/56	
60887	887	4858	30/11/39	6/7/64		
60888	888	4859	7/12/39	29/12/62		
60889	889	4860	17/12/39	11/6/63	MC3/61	
60890	890	4861	28/12/39	30/4/62		
60891	891	4862	29/12/39	12/10/64	MC1/57	

60892	892	4863	11/1/40	21/11/63		
60893	893	4864	20/1/40	23/9/62	MC5/60	
60894	894	4865	20/1/40	29/12/62		
60895	795/895	4866	26/1/40	4/10/65		
60896	896	4867	3/2/40	23/9/62		
60897	897	4868	10/2/40	11/6/63	SA9/60	
60898	898	4869	22/2/40	28/11/63		
60899	799/899	4870	23/2/40	22/9/63	SC8/51, SA9/60, MC8/61	
60900	900	4871	2/3/40	11/4/63	SC2/46	
60901	901	4872	9/3/40	14/6/65	SC2/46, MC9/57	
60902	902	4873	15/3/40	22/9/63	DBK10/61	
60903	903/E903	4874	20/3/40	10/2/63	SC10/53, DBK8/61	
60904	904	4875	3/4/40	9/7/64	MC7/57	
60905	805/905	4876	10/4/40	22/9/63	MC10/59	
60906	906	4877	17/4/40	28/5/63	MC12/60	
60907	907	4878	19/4/40	28/5/62	SC11/53	
60908	908	4879	29/4/40	4/6/62		
60909	809/909	4880	4/5/40	8/6/62	SC8/51	
60910	910	4881	10/5/40	15/4/64	MC10/59	
60911	911	4882	15/5/40	3/12/62		
60912	912/E912	4883	24/5/40	29/4/63	SC3/54, MC10/61	
60913	913	4884	6/6/40	12/10/64	MC5/59	
60914	914	4885	14/6/40	23/9/62	SC5/52, MC8/58	
60915	915	4886	15/6/40	25/11/62		
60916	916	4887	24/7/40	26/6/64		
60917	917	4888	10/8/40	13/4/62		
60918	918	4889	28/8/41	8/10/62	SC9/51	
60919	919	4890	7/9/41	2/9/66		
60920	920	4891	4/10/41	29/12/62		
60921	921	4892	16/10/41	11/6/63		
60922	922	4893	31/10/41	9/7/62		
60923	923	4894	15/11/41	4/10/65	MC1/57	
60924	924/E924	4895	22/11/41	22/9/63		
60925	925	4896	4/12/41	25/5/64	SC8/52	
60926	926	4897	17/12/41	1/10/62		
60927	927	4898	20/12/41	3/12/62		
60928	928	3655	24/6/41	5/3/62		DR1921
60929	929	3656	25/6/41	21/6/65	SC1/54, MC11/60	DR1922
60930	930	3657	26/7/41	23/9/62	SC1/54	DR1923
60931	931	3658	23/8/41	3/9/65	MC12/58	DR1924
60932	932	3659	22/10/41	25/5/64	MC9/58	DR1925
60933	933	3660	23/10/41	29/12/62		DR1926
60934	934	3661	7/1/42	22/10/62	SC9/51	DR1927
60935	935	3662	17/2/42	7/6/63	MC9/61	DR1928
60936	936	3663	3/3/42	23/9/62	MC3/60	DR1929
60937	937/E937	3664	9/3/42	29/12/62		DR1930
60938	938	4899	29/1/42	1/10/62		
60939	939	3641	12/2/42	12/10/64	SC8/51	
60940	940	3642	21/2/42	11/10/65	MC9/56	
60941	941	3643	4/3/42	6/7/64	SC11/52	
60942	942	3644	13/3/42	25/5/64	SC7/52, MC12/56	
60943	943	3645	26/3/42	23/9/62	MC9/60	
60944	944	3646	17/4/42	20/9/65		
60945	945	3647	15/5/42	6/7/64	MC3/57	
60946	946	3648	21/5/42	11/10/65		
60947	947	3649	3/6/42	1/10/62		
60948	948	3650	11/6/42	22/9/63	SA12/60, MC12/61	
60949	949	3651	18/6/42	25/11/62		
60950	950	3652	26/6/42	22/9/63	SA12/60, MC9/60	
60951	951	3653	7/7/42	29/12/62		
60952	952	3654	18/7/42	11/10/65		
60953	953	3665	26/8/42	28/5/62		
60954	954	3666	5/9/42	18/11/63	SC8/51	
60955	955	3667	22/9/42	26/9/66		
60956	956	3668	30/9/42	23/9/62	SC5/52, MC9/59	
60957	957/E957	3669	7/10/42	17/12/64	SC9/53, MC6/57	
60958	958/E958	3670	15/10/42	29/12/62		
60959	959	3671	2/11/42	1/7/63		
60960	960	3672	11/11/42	26/2/62	SC12/52	
60961	961	3673	2/12/42	5/4/65		
60962	962	3674	23/12/42	20/9/65		
60963	963	3675	12/1/43	29/6/65	DB2/60	DN1903
60964	964	3676	26/1/43	8/5/64	NM29/4/58, MC1/60	DN1904
60965	965	3677	25/2/43	29/12/62		DN1905
60966	966	3678	15/3/43	11/6/63	SC7/51	DN1906
60967	967	3679	26/3/43	10/2/64	SC9/51, SC9/53, MC11/58	DN1907
60968	968	3680	15/4/43	20/5/63	SC9/51, SC2/54, MC4/61	DN1908
60969	969	3681	29/4/43	18/5/64	MC6/60	DN1909
60970	970	3682	12/5/43	7/2/66	MC4/60	DN1910
60971	871/971	3683	2/6/43	29/12/62		DN1911
60972	972	3684	1/7/43	28/11/63		DN1913
60973	973	3685	24/7/43	24/1/66		DN1914
60974	974	3686	19/8/43	9/12/63		DN1915
60975	975	3687	20/9/43	25/5/64		DN1917
60976	976	3688	7/10/43	26/9/66	MC8/60	DN1918
60977	977	3689	27/10/43	26/2/62	SC1/54	DN1919
60978	978	3690	9/12/43	19/11/62		DN1921
60979	979	3691	20/1/44	1/10/62	SC7/52	DN1923
60980	980	3692	10/3/44	29/12/62		DN1926
60981	981	3693	20/4/44	15/4/63	SC7/46	DN1929
60982	982	3694	21/6/44	5/10/64		DN1935
60983	983	3695	13/7/44	23/9/62		DN1936
61700	1700	3401	25/2/41	14/3/57	Named BANTAM COCK	DR1919
61701	1701	3402	21/3/41	26/11/57	Thermic siphon removed 6/45	DR1920

KEY TO APPENDIX B

NM Named
MC Separate cylinder castings
DF Trial smoke deflector fitted
DB BR double blastpipe fitted
DBK Kylchap double blastpipe fitted
NMX Name chosen but not used.
MS MLS multiple valve regulator fitted when new.
SW Tested at Swindon 1952-3
SC Self-cleaning apparatus fitted (various)
SA Spark arrestor used
ST Stepped tender side coupled when new
CC Copper capped chimney carried
DN Darlington Works
DR Doncaster Works

APPENDIX C PUBLISHED PERFORMANCES

LOCO	Tons LOAD	MILES	Minutes SCHED	Minutes ACTUAL	Minutes NET	MPH ACTUAL	MPH NET	D/U
KINGS CROSS - PETERBOROUGH								
60800	320	76.35	87	83.48	75.00	54.87	61.08	D
60800	415	76.35	86	89.27	78.00	51.32	58.73	U
60817	365	76.35	81	74.60	69.50	61.41	65.91	U
60817	360	76.35	83	74.58	73.00	61.42	62.75	U
60828	550	76.35	91	84.55	77.00	54.18	59.49	U
60866	360	76.35	85	86.33	80.00	53.06	57.26	D
60869	385	76.35	88	82.93	82.93	55.24	55.24	D
60880	400	76.35	81	81.90	73.50	55.93	62.33	U
60903	425	76.35	90	98.00	80.50	46.74	56.91	U
60912	525	76.35	91	86.12	83.00	53.19	55.19	U
60935	215	76.35	72	73.90	70.00	61.99	65.44	U
60950	450	76.35	90	83.60	77.00	54.80	59.49	U
PETERBOROUGH - GRANTHAM								
60800	415	29.10	33	41.47	32.50	42.11	53.72	U
60828	410	29.10	33	30.87	29.25	56.57	59.69	U
60828	525	29.10	38	33.07	32.50	52.80	53.72	U
60828	550	29.10	34	33.83	33.83	51.61	51.61	U
60901	525	29.10	34	36.70	32.00	47.57	54.56	U
60903	425	29.10	30	47.32	34.00	36.90	51.35	U
60950	450	29.10	30	30.82	30.82	56.66	56.66	U
60956	430	29.10	33	29.97	29.97	58.26	58.26	U
KINGS CROSS - GRANTHAM								
60814	390	105.45	123	121.08	115.00	52.25	55.02	D
60858	460	105.45	121	109.77	107.00	57.64	59.13	D
60897	430	105.45	122	124.93	115.00	50.64	55.02	D
60943	490	105.45	127	118.17	107.00	53.54	59.13	U
60956	475	105.45	119	124.70	112.00	50.74	56.49	D
GRANTHAM - DONCASTER								
60837	410	50.60	62	61.00	60.50	49.77	50.18	D
60884	425	50.60	61	71.93	60.00	42.21	50.60	U
60897	445	50.60	62	61.51	57.00	49.36	53.26	D
60943	345	50.60	58	63.50	63.00	47.81	48.19	U

LOCO	Tons LOAD	MILES	Minutes SCHED	Minutes ACTUAL	Minutes NET	MPH ACTUAL	MPH NET	D/U
KINGS CROSS - LEEDS CENTRAL (WEST RIDING LIMITED)								
60818	295	185.70	163	167.00	167.00	66.72	66.72	D
60872	550	185.70	241	277.58	237.00	40.14	47.01	U
PETERBOROUGH - DONCASTER								
60893	510	79.20	88	90.05	84.00	52.77	56.57	U
PETERBOROUGH - YORK								
60936	385	111.80	126	127.10	120.00	52.78	55.90	D
PETERBOROUGH - NEWCASTLE								
60869	405	191.90	204	200.53	200.53	57.42	57.42	D
YORK - DARLINGTON								
60835	245	44.15	41	38.45	39.45	68.89	67.15	U
NEWCASTLE - EDINBURGH								
60933	345	124.45	167	161.16	150.50	46.33	49.61	D
CARLISLE - EDINBURGH								
60937	260	98.10	152	158.62	145.50	37.11	40.45	D
PERTH - ABERDEEN								
60898	335	89.80	105	109.63	105.00	49.15	51.31	U
60955	260	89.80	93	96.55	91.50	55.81	58.89	U
DUNDEE - ABERDEEN								
60851	395	71.30	100	97.12	91.50	44.05	46.75	U

APPENDIX D NOTABLE V2 PERFORMANCES

LOCOMOTIVE	60022			60004		
CHANGED TO	60946			60852		
TRAIN	8.00dep Newcastle			9.45 dep Edinburgh		
LOAD	363/385			363/385		
DATE	12/10/1957			29/8/58		
LOCATION	TIME	+/-		TIME	+/-	
Newcastle dep	8.00	RT		11.55	pass 4-	
Durham arr	8.18	RT		pass		
Durham dep	8.20	RT		12.11	4-	
Ferryhill	8.33	RT	TSR			
Darlington arr	8.47	RT		pass		
dep	8.49	RT		12.33	4-	
Northallerton	9.03	RT		12.45	4-	
York arr	9.31	RT		pass		
dep	9.36	RT		13.11	4-	
Shaftholme Jct	10.12	2-	Sigs Moss	13.39	RT	
Doncaster arr	10.11	4BT		13.43	RT	
CHANGE LOCO dep	10.25	10-		13.51	8-	
Retford	10.46	12.5	TSR	14.09	9-	Sigs 20
Newark	11.06	15-	TSR mp128	14.26	9-	
Grantham	11.20	12-		14.39	9-	
Peterborough	11.45	7-		15.04	5-	
Huntingdon	12.02	6.5-		15.19	2-	
Hitchin	12.26	3-		15.40	RT	
Hatfield	12.39	2-		15.52	2 +	
Finsbury Park	12.52	8BT		16.15	RT	8 min sigs P. Bar
Kings Cross	12.57	8BT		16.20	RT	
Doncaster-Kings +						
Booked	170			158		
Gross	152			149		
Net	145.5			138		

APPENDIX D FAST RUNNING 1. Grantham-Kings Cross

Loco	60800		60828		60943		60950	
Load	380/415		497/550		490		450	
Driver	Rowe		Walcome		Arrend			
Date	22/1/55		23/1/54		Aug 1957		6/5/05	
	min.sec		min.sec		min.sec		min.sec	
GRANTHAM	0 .0		0.0		0.0		0.0	
Gt Ponton	9.19	TSR	8.20	33			7.42	
Stoke	13.9	39	11.30	40	10.6	46	10.37	41
Corby Glen	16.43	66	15.0	63	13.2	73	13.46	
Little Bytham	20.42	88	19.0	70	16.37	91	17.45	
Essendine	23.02	97	21.55	78	18.56	94	20.23	85
Tallington	25.27	92	25.1	81max	21.28	91	23.14	
Werrington Jct	30.27	Fog 60	29.43		25.43	55	27.20	
PETERBOROUGH	41.28	Sigs	33.50		31.25	PSR 20	30.49	
	0 0		0.0		0.0		0.0	
Fletton Jct	3.33		3.24				2.25	
Yaxley	6.58		6.30	51			6.23	
Holme	10.8	68	9.41	70	41.7	72	9.31	67
Abbots Ripton	15.43	58	15.33	52	46.14	64	15.13	53.5
Huntingdon North	20.10	70	20.11	66	50.30	68	19.48	74
Offord	22.39		22.35	72	53.8	73/TSR	22.13	
St Neots	26.35	68	26.8	82	59.3	44/48	25.55	61
Tempsford	30.23	72	29.48	70	63.26	74	29.28	72.5
Sandy	33.19	70	32.40	73	66.25	70	32.34	62.5
Biggleswade	35.55	69	35.15	66	69.2	66	35.13	72.5
Arlesey	39.39	71	39.2	65	72.40	76	39.3	61/66
Three Counties	40.44				73.40	74		
HITCHIN	44.16	65	43.53	62	77.10	62/60	44.1	53.5
Stevenage	47.50	52	47.33	46	80.42	58	48.1	47
Knebworth	51.25	Sig stop			83.55	68		
Woolmer Green	55.11		52.53	Sigs 50	85.28	Sigs 60	53.32	
Welwyn North	58.58	Sigs	54.28	Sigs 55	86.53	69/72		
Welwyn Gdn City	62.20		56.19		88.19	74	56.25	
Hatfield	65.19		59.0		90.39		58.50	66
Potters Bar	71.18	TSR 20	65.1	TSR 10	95.44	60	64.0	
New Barnet	77.8		70.28		99.18	67/71	67.13	
Wood Green	81.17		74.48		103.28	66	70.51	Sigs
Finsbury Park	84.18		77.23	Sig stop	107.11	Sigs	73.29	Sig stop
KINGS CROSS	89.16		84.33		118.10	Sigs	83.36	Sigs
Schedule	(33+86) 119.0		(34+91) 125.0		121.0		(30+90) 120.0	
Net time	(32.5+78) 110.5		(33.8+77) 110.8		107.0		(30.8+77) 107.8	

APPENDIX D FAST RUNNING
2. Kings Cross-Grantham

Loco 60858			
Load 465			
Date 2/8/57	Min	Sec	Speed
KINGS CROSS	0	0	
Finsbury Park	8	6	
Wood Green	11	26	55/60
New Barnet	16	4	53
Potters Bar	20	6	52
Hatfield	24	51	70/76
Welwyn Gdn City	27	4	70
Welwyn North	28	42	65
Woolmer Green	30	8	62
Knebworth	31	46	58/61
Stevenage	35	9	63/65
HITCHIN	38	3	74
Three Counties	41	1	80
Arlesey	42	6	76
Biggleswade	45	40	71
Sandy	48	25	TSR 40
Tempsford	51	50	68
St Neots	55	40	68/70
Offord	59	18	74/71
Huntingdon North	61	57	69
Abbots Ripton	66	32	60
Holme	71	17	80/71
Yaxley	74	1	68
Fletton Jct	76	18	
PETERBOROUGH	78	22	PSR 20
Werrington Jct	83	37	
Tallington	88	37	68
Essendine	91	54	72
Little Bytham	95	1	70/68
Corby Glen	99	59	57/62
Stoke	103	15	55
Gt Ponton	105	14	TSR 20
GRANTHAM	109	46	
Schedule	121		
Net time	107		

637 GREEN ARROW in works grey with the original curved nameplate, Doncaster Works.

APPENDIX E. PEAK PERIOD OPERATIONS
Summer Holiday Peak
Down Service Saturday 30 July and Friday 5 August 1955

DEPARTURE	TO	30/7/55 ENGINE	DEPARTURE	5/8/55 ENGINE
16.45	Newcastle	60008		
2.45	Grantham	60014	2.45	60903
3.50	Leeds	60881	3.50	60003
5.15	York	60021	5.15	60010
7.55	Skegness	61177	7.50	60120
8.05	Skegness	61073		
8.10	Filey Camp	60067		
8.20	York	60153	8.20	60146
9.00	Newcastle	60108	9.00	60108
9.18	Leeds/Bradford	60141	9.18	60025
9.30	Edinburgh	60011	9.30	60031
9.40	Newcastle	60027	9.40	60148
9.50	Edinburgh	60039		
10.00	Edinburgh	60125	10.00	60008
10.04	Glasgow	60983		
10.10	Glasgow	60078	10.05	60508
10.17	Leeds/Bradford	60966	10.17	60842
10.28	Hull	60914		
10.34	Leeds/Bradford	60862		
10.40	Grantham	60876	10.40	60500
10.45	Leeds/Bradford	60030	10.50	60026
10.54	Leeds	60015		
10.55	Skegness	61203		
11.20	Scarborough	60908	11.20	60903
11.30	Glasgow	60872		
11.40	Newcastle	60832	11.40	60032
12.05	Glasgow	60134	12.05	60131
12.10	Newcastle	60017	12.10	60046
12.17	Newcastle	60049	12.18	60033
12.25	Newcastle	60013		
12.35	Leeds/Bradford	60109	12.35	60842
12.38	Peterborough	60906		
12.45	Edinburgh	60518		
12.55	Leeds/Bradford	60843		
13.05	Leeds/Bradford	60865	13.05	60029
13.17	Leeds/Bradford	60026	13.18	60064
13.30	Hull	60917		
13.45	Edinburgh	60924	13.45	60924
14.00	Edinburgh	60513	14.00	60513
	Hull		14.10	60049
14.18	Leeds	60014	14.18	60862
15.00	Newcastle	60110	15.00	60110
15.10	Newcastle	60903		
15.20	Newcastle	60149	15.20	60125
15.45	Leeds	60117	15.45	60117
15.49	Leeds	61031	15.50	60014
15.55	Leeds	60055		
15.59	Cleethorpes	61082	15.59	60055
16.15	Cleethorpes	61182	16.10	61318
16.15	Peterborough	60826	16.15	60874
16.45	Newcastle	SX	16.45	60147
17.00	Peterborough	60063	17.00	60017
17.30	Leeds	60007	17.30	60007
17.34	Newcastle	60114	17.34	60903
17.50	Newcastle	(60515)	17.50	60149
18.10	Leeds	60875	18.05	60533
18.18	Leeds	60123	18.18	60141
18.40	Grimsby Town	61318	18.40	61182
			18.45	60056
			18.50	60850
19.00	Aberdeen	60144	19.00	60128
19.15	Aberdeen	60053	19.15	60063
19.15	York 102 Pcls	60852	19.15	60935
19.21	Peterborough	60062	19.21	60030
			20.10	60876
20.20	Edinburgh	60533	20.20	60021
			21.55	60121
22.15	Edinburgh	60129	22.15	60003
22.20	Edinburgh	60515	22.20	60983
22.35	Edinburgh	60064	22.35	60026
22.45	Edinburgh	60914	22.45	60112
23.00	Leeds	60008	23.00	60006
23.45	Newcastle	60125	23.45	60148
			23.50	60869
			Spl	43081
14.50 262 Frt	Edinb'gh Niddrie	SX	14.50	60832
15.15 266 Frt	Edinb'gh Niddrie	60800	15.15	60905
16.16 714 Frt	York D'houses	60803	16.15	60914
18.20SO/19.15 1224 frt	Leeds Goods	SX	18.20 SO/19.15	60861
20.15 660 Frt	York D'houses	SX	20.15	60979
20.25 666 Frt	Hull Hessle Yd	SX	20.25	61075
21.15 1266 Frt	Leeds Goods	60861	21.15	60865
L E	Grimsby Town	61374	LE	
1202 GDS SO	Colwick	61902	SO	
22.25 1252GDS	Colwick	60506	22.25	61816

Summer Holiday Peak
Up Service Saturday 30 July and Friday 5 August 1955

ARRIVAL	FROM	30/7/55 ENGINE	ARRIVAL	5/8/55 ENGINE
			00.50	60030
3.04	Newcastle	60153	3.04	60146
6.10	Edinburgh	60125		
6.20	Edinburgh	60065	6.20	60148
6.40	Dundee	60129	6.40	60147
7.00	Aberdeen	60966	7.00	60508
7.40	Aberdeen	60078	7.40	60500
			9.00	60881
9.52	Grantham	60014	9.52	60903
10.35	Peterborough	60906	10.35	60842
10.45	Newcastle Pcls	60917	10.45	60870
10.45	Grimsby Town	61318	10.45	61182
10.50	Nottingham	60881	10.50	60003
11.06	Leeds	61031		
11.20	Leeds	60021	11.20	60010
11.35	Doncaster	60826		
11.41	Bradford	60148	11.50	60117
11.59	Skegness	61374		
12.07	Leeds	60056		
12.15	Leeds	60117		
12.16	Peterborough	60513	12.16	60832
12.32	Hull	60064	12.32	60055
12.47	Darlington	60110		
12.55	Cambridge	60062	12.59	60030
12.59	York/Hull	60055		
13.09	Grimsby Town	61082		
13.18	Newcastle	60803	13.18	60874
13.28	Newcastle	60895	13.25	60125
13.35	Newcastle	60149		
13.40	Cleethorpes	61182	13.40	61318
			13.42	60874
13.50	Saltburn	60975	13.50	60021
13.58	Newcastle	60008	13.58	60006
14.05	Newcastle	60114		
14.15	Leeds/Brfd	60025	14.15	60925
14.30	Newcastle	60515		
14.37	Hull/Harrogate	60123	14.37	60141
14.58	Scarborough	60003		
15.07	Sth Shields	60053	15.07	60533
15.30	Newcastle	60144	15.30	60149
15.37	Skegness	61073		
15.40	Leeds	60875		
15.50	Bradford/Ripon	60015		
15.53	Leeds/Brfd	60966	15.53	60803
16.00	Bradford/Ripon	60030		
16.07	Filey Camp	60106		
16.18	Peterborough	61207	16.10	61202
16.19	Hull	60909	16.15	61073
16.30	Edinburgh	60033	16.15	60034
			16.20	60128
17.12	Newcastle	60034	17.12	60501
17.28	Edinburgh	60914	17.28	60121
17.50	Leeds/Brfd	60908	17.50	60903
17.57	Scarborough	60017	17.57	60032
18.05	Hull/Harrogate	60876	18.06	60026
			18.20	60866
18.32	Glasgow	60872	18.32	60029
18.40	Skegness*	61203		
19.15	Hull	60049		
19.30	Newcastle	60108	19.30	60064
19.33	Leeds/Brfd	60013	19.33	60112
19.40	Leeds/Brfd	60026	19.40	60033
19.50	Glasgow	60141	19.50	60120
20.03	Peterborough	60862	20.03	60829
21.15	Skegness	61047	20.55	60049
21.30	Leeds/Hull	60103	21.32	60134
21.35	Leeds/Brfd	60865		
21.40	Leeds/Brfd	60014	21.40	60862
21.48	Glasgow	60156	21.50	60125
21.58	Edinburgh	60125	21.58	60148
22.10FRI	Leeds/Brfd	60134	22.10	60118
			22.20	60067
8.55 275 Frt	Edinburgh Niddrie	SX	8.55	60979
16.35 273 Frt	Inverkeithing	SX	16.35	60876
20.35 1113 Frt	Doncaster	60948	20.35	61977
22.40 581 Frt	Hull Hessle	61075	22.40	61203
22.40 1271 Frt	New Clee	SX	22.40	61912
22.55 1297 Frt	New Clee	SX	22.55	61825
23.55 39up ECS	Peterborough	60063	23.55	60017

Side-on in works grey again; note how
the plate does not match the wheel.

APPENDIX E. OPERATIONS AT GRANTHAM 15 December 1954

DOWN Dep K+	TO	FROM KINGS +	FROM GRANTHAM	UP Arr K+	FROM	TO GRANTHAM	TO KINGS +
2.45	Grantham	60007		3.04	Newcastle		(60524)
3.50	Leeds	60014		6.20	Edinburgh		60158
5.15	York	60033		6.40	Dundee		60875*
8.20	York	60524*	61094 (arr)	7.15	Aberdeen		60500
9.00	Newcastle	60062	(60062)	7.40	Aberdeen		60850
9.18	Leeds/Bradford	60026	60026	9.50	Grantham		60007
	Edinburgh	From PE	60925	10.35	Peterborough		60874
9.50	Edinburgh	60866	60514		Relief 103 Pcls		60105
10.00	Edinburgh	60158	60144	10.45	Newcastle 103 Pcls		60897
10.04	Glasgow	60500	60912	10.45	Grimsby Town		61130
10.10	Glasgow	60850	60538	10.50	Nottingham		60014
10.17	Leeds/Bradford	60022	60130	11.10	Leeds RLF	(60141)	60141
10.28	Hull	60906	60119	11.20	Leeds	(60130)	60033
10.40	Grantham	60025		11.30	Doncaster RLF	(60064)	60064
10.50	Leeds	60008	61392	11.40	Leeds	(60139)	60139
12.40 GRA	Doncaster		60113	11.50	Leeds	(60120)	60120
11.40	Newcastle	60828	60810	12.15	Hull	60905	60905
12.05	Glasgow	60123	60123	12.32	Hull	60889	60889
12.10	Newcastle	60121	60839	12.47	Darlington	60810	60122
12.18	Newcastle	60903	60083	12.59	York/Hull	60055	60055
12.35	Leeds/Bradford	60010	60010	13.09	Grimsby Town		(61311)
12.45	Leeds/Bradford	60914	60520	13.15	Newcastle	60127	60523PE
12.55	Leeds/Bradford	60859	60859	13.25	Newcastle	60839	60139
13.05	Leeds/Bradford	60902	60513	13.35	Newcastle	60083	60157
13.18	Leeds/Bradford	60826	60131	13.40	Cleethorpes		(61082)
13.25	Leeds/Bradford	60052	60052	13.50	Leeds	60015	60015
13.30	Edinburgh	60893	60930	14.00	Leeds	60030	60030
13.45	Edinburgh	60921	60866 PE	14.15	Newcastle	60023	60023
13.54	Edinburgh	60869	60078 PE	14.37	Hull/Harrogate	60133	60133
14.00	Edinburgh	60122	60845 PE	14.58	Leeds	60520	60103
14.10	Edinburgh	60007	60127 PE	15.07	Newcastle	60853	60109
14.18	Leeds/Hull	60905		15.30	Newcastle	60056	60125
14.50	Newcastle	60983	60520	15.40	Leeds/Bradford	60930	60158
15.00	Newcastle	60875		15.50	Bradford/Ripon	60131	60149
15.10	Newcastle	60523		15.53	Leeds/Brfd	60865	60865
From PE	Newcastle		60002	16.00	Bradford/Ripon	60026	60026
15.20	Newcastle	60157		16.10	Grimsby Town	61143	60906
15.45	Leeds/Bradford	60120	60120	16.15	Peterborough		61070
16.10	Grimsby Town	61311		16.20	Lincoln	K3	60008
15.50	Leeds/Bradford	60055	60055	16.30	Leeds/Hull	60508	60022
15.59	Leeds/Bradford	60139	60139	273 Frt	Inverkeithing	60911	60911
16.05	Hull	60067	60067	23F56	Troop Spl	60886	60828
16.15	Peterborough	60866		23F57	Troop Spl	60956	60121
16.20	Cleethorpes	61082		23F58	Troop Spl	60952	60914
16.45	Newcastle	60014	60014	17.12	Newcastle	60080	60936 PE
17.00	Peterborough	60800		17.28	Edinburgh	60143	60025
17.30	Leeds/Hull	60032	60032	18.05	Glasgow	60124	60921 PE
17.34	Newcastle	60862	(60143)	18.32	Glasgow	60533	60007 PE
17.50	Newcastle	60125	60132	19.15	Hull	60877	60877
18.05	Leeds/Hull	60141	(60141)	19.30	Leeds/Brfd	60871	60871
18.18	Leeds/Hull	60133	(60133)	19.33	Leeds/Brfd	60039	60826
18.40	Grimsby Town	61130		19.40	Leeds/Brfd	60916	60903
19.00	Aberdeen	60149	(60149)	19.50	Glasgow	60118	60118
19.15	Aberdeen	60158	(60158)	581 Frt	Hull Hessle	61075	61075
19.21	Peterborough			1113 Frt	Doncaster Decoy	60870	60870
20.20	Edinburgh TPO	60030		21.32	Leeds/Brfd		
22.15	Edinburgh	60023	(60023)	21.40	Leeds/Brfd	(60026)	(60026)
22.20	Edinburgh			21.58	Edinburgh		(60157)
22.35	Edinburgh	(60022)		22.10	Leeds/Brfd	(60123)	(60123)
22.45	Edinburgh	(60025)		39upECS	Peterborough		(60800)
23.00	Leeds/Hull						
23.45	Newcastle	(60157)					
12.35	York 842Pcls	60874					
19.15	York 102Pcls	60112	(60112)				
498Frt	Doncaster Decoy	60896	(60896)				
266Frt	Edinburgh Niddrie	60899	(60899)				
1224Frt	Leeds Goods	60861	(60861)				
1266Frt	Leeds Goods	60865	(60865)				
666Frt	Hull Hessle	61364	(61364)				
1252Frt	Colwick	61974	(61974)				
( ) Assumed							
* Failure							

APPENDIX E. NIGHT FREIGHT 16/17 July 1954

TIME	DESTINATION	CLASS	LOCO
17.34	Saltburn	A	60015
17.50	Newcastle	A	60128
18.10	Hull/Ripon	A	60113
18.18	Leeds/Bradford	A	60118
18.45	Aberdeen	A	60109
19.00	Aberdeen	A	60125
19.15	Aberdeen	A	60056
19.21	Peterborough	B	60103
19.25	102 York Parcels	C	60046
19.15	1224 Leeds Goods	C	60846
20.00	Cambridge	A	61671
20.10	Newcastle	A	60140
20.20	Edinburgh TPO	A	60029
20.15	660 York Dringhouses	C	60963
20.25	666 Hull Hessle Yd	C	61394
21.15	1266 Leeds Goods	D	60928
21.55	Edinburgh	A	60010
22.15	Edinburgh	A	60154
22.20	Edinburgh	A	60047
22.35	Edinburgh	A	60034
22.45	Newc'le/Bradford	A	60815
23.00	Bradford	A	60022
23.00	122 York Parcels	C	60911
23.35	Newcastle	A	60157
23.45	Newcastle	A	60149
23.30	524 York	D	60855
23.40	890 Boston Parcels	C	61203
00.05	1016 Doncaster Decoy	D	60893
00.55	Edinburgh	A	60513
00.45	New Clee	D	61825
23.05	1290 Lincoln Holmes	D	61113
01.15	520 Heaton	D	61800
02.05	268 Niddrie	C	60914
SPL	York	E	61392
SPL	New England	E	61282
02.20	1062 New England	H	61095
02.34	Grantham news/pcls	C	60821
03.50	Leeds	A	60006
05.15	24 York news/pcls	C	60062
05.45	Doncaster	A	60158
06.53	Grantham	A	60128
	2452 Southgate pilot	J	64196
08.00	Skegness	A	61122
08.05	Skegness	A	61138
08.20	Filey Camp	A	60146
09.00	Newcastle TCQ	A	60026
09.10	Leeds/Bradford	A	60131
09.30	Edinburgh	A	60009
09.40	Edinburgh	A	60014
09.50	Edinburgh	A	(60909)
10.00	Edinburgh	A	60149

TIME	ORIGIN	CLASS	LOCO
19.33	Doncaster	A	60815
19.40	Leeds/Bradford	A	60030
19.50	Glasgow	A	60131
20.35	1113 Doncaster Decoy	E Bkd	60889
20.03	Peterborough	B	61093
20.40	581 Hessle	C	61393
21.32	Leeds/Bradford	A	60053
21.48	Glasgow	A	60006
21.40	Leeds/Bradford	A	61027*
21.50	Edinburgh	A	60149
22.05	Bradford	A	60133
22.27	1271 New Clee	C	61825
22.55	1297 New Clee	C	61800
00.15	39 ECS Newcastle	C	60014
00.35	1321 Doncaster Decoy	D	60160
00.50	1325 Colwick	C	61821
01.00	589 Hull	C	60829
01.10	1359 Grimsby	C	61095
01.50	1369 New England	D	60103
SPL	255 York	C	61392
01.30	935 Wakefield Pcls	C	60123
02.15	611 York	C	61139
02.40	259 Aberdeen	C	60026
03.04	Newcastle	A	60146
03.15	Leeds/Bradford	A	60861
03.40	1343 Leeds Goods	C	60134
03.55	261 Aberdeen	C	60962
04.03	Leeds/Bradford	A	60158
04.15	881 Doncaster-Hornsey	C	60853
04.15	Newcastle	A	61138
04.25	Leeds/Bradford/Hull	A	60909
04.35	Newcastle	A	60128
04.50	South Shields	A	60010
05.05	Newcastle	A	60047
05.05	591 Hull	C	60867
05.40	1355 Lincoln Holmes	D	60034
05.55	Edinburgh	A	60022
06.10	Edinburgh	A	60015
06.20	Edinburgh	A	60149
06.30	715 Boston	C	60950
06.40	Dundee	A	60005
07.00	Aberdeen	A	60504
07.40	Aberdeen	A	60505
07.55	555 Newcastle Forth	C	60828
SPL	441	A	60145
SPL	443	A	60821
SPL	458	A	60916
SPL	462	A	60029
SPL	501	A	60148
SPL	505	A	60905
09.50	Grantham	A	(60047)

TIMETABLED SERVICES CANCELLED			
19.15	1232	F	WD
19.15	1234	H	WD
21.25	1268	H	WD
22.00	1256	F	WD
22.30	1242	E UB	WD
23.05	1290	D	WD
00.45	1018	H	WD
01.30	1054	H	WD
02.40	1048	F	WD
03.10	1064	H	WD
04.20	1068	H	WD
04.50	1078	F	WD
07.15	1090	H	WD
	(All to New England)		

1287	New England	H	WD
1291	New England	E Bkd	
1299	Long Sutton	D	
1305	New England	H	WD
1303	Boston	D	WD
1365	Firsby	D	WD
1379	New England	F	WD
257	Aberdeen	C	V2
1021	New England	E Bkd	
261	Aberdeen	C	V2
1017	Colwick	C	

The 'Books of' the LNER 4-6-2s and 2-6-2s concluded. Spot the V2...

Alec Swain, www.transporttreasury.co.uk